PRAISE FOR *WHO DO YOU S*

Whenever Jesus made a *Great I Am* statement, His friends were in awe, and His enemies wanted to stone Him, because those words were a clear declaration of deity. The *I Am*s are the jewels of John's gospel, and Becky Harling does an excellent job of helping you see how to apply them to your real-life challenges.

DEE BRESTIN
Author of *The Friendships of Women* and *He Calls You Beautiful*

In *Who Do You Say That I AM?* Becky Harling reminds us of eight powerful questions Jesus asked in the Gospels that have a profound impact on our lives. Gather a group of your friends, and discover the rich experience of studying these questions together. Discussing the life applications, praising Him, and memorizing Scripture will transform your thinking.

CAROL KENT
Speaker and author of *He Holds Your Hand: Experiencing God's Presence and Protection*

I appreciate that each lesson in this study begins with a question Jesus asked—like "Do you want to get well?" or "Can you add to your life by worrying?" or "Why are you so afraid?"—because these are my questions too. And probably yours. The good news is that Becky Harling provides the answers that will take us deeper into the heart of God and enable us to live an "abundant adventure"—beyond the questions.

LUCINDA SECREST MCDOWELL
Author of *Ordinary Graces*

With authentic and inspiring stories from her own life and the lives of others, Becky Harling gently invites us to go from merely knowing Jesus to longing for deep intimacy with Him. This study draws you in to boldly answer the questions Jesus poses in the Gospels to His followers. I highly recommend this Bible study for your church or small group to help grow strong followers of Christ.

CYNTHIA CAVANAUGH
Speaker, life coach, and author of the *Live Unveiled Bible Study* and *Anchored: Leading Through the Storms*

ecky Harling invites us to journey through the Gospels and discover with fresh eyes who Jesus is—not only in church history but also in our hectic, heartache-prone lives. Through sound biblical insight and encouragement, *Who Do You Say That I AM?* delivers the kind of truth that can heal weary souls and lead us to a deeper faith in Christ.

BECKY KOPITZKE
Author of *Generous Love: Discover the Joy of Living "Others First"* and *The SuperMom Myth: Conquering the Dirty Villains of Motherhood*

Oh, how I love the divine truths that are found on the sacred pages of the Bible! In *Who Do You Say That I AM?* Becky Harling has created a study of God's Word that is alive with hope, depth, and vivid revelation. As you join your heart with the knowledge of who Jesus is, you will become more and more like Him.

CAROL MCLEOD
Bestselling author and Bible teacher
CEO of Just Joy! Ministries
Host of Defiant Joy! Radio and a Jolt of Joy

If you are longing for a fresh encounter with Jesus, *Who Do You Say That I AM?* will reignite your heart and stir your affections for Jesus. More than a Bible study, each lesson provides poignant teaching and thought-provoking questions that nourish your soul and lead you on a deeper journey in your faith.

LISA BISHOP
Director of Women's Ministries, Park Community Church, Chicago

This is a powerful, life-changing study, and anyone who has ever faced fear or doubt can walk away certain of God's power to perform His Word. Becky Harling's study shares the victories available to all who trust and know the *Great I Am.*

EVELYN JOHNSON-TAYLOR
Founder of Women of Promise International Ministries Inc.
Author, speaker, theology professor

Becky Harling helps you find the biblical, practical, and transformational answers to the vital question Christ asked: "Who do you say that I am?" Calm comes, power is given, and victories unfold. That is what awaits you!

PAM FARREL
International speaker, author of many books including bestselling *Men Are Like Waffles, Women Are Like Spaghetti* and *Discovering Hope In the Psalms.*

Understanding who Jesus is—I mean, who He really, truly is—changes everything. Answers questions. Inspires. Bolsters. Comforts. Delivers. Blesses! Becky Harling packages all that and more and ties it up with a beautifully biblical bow in *Who Do You Say That I AM?*

RHONDA RHEA
TV personality, humor columnist, author of many books, including *Messy to Meaningful, Turtles in the Road* and *Fix-Her-Upper*

As a pastor's wife and ministry leader, I have women come to me in search of answers about faith issues, such as, if God is who He says He is, where is He during life's disappointments? I've had a few questions of my own over the years. This study helped me discover who I am because of knowing the *Great I Am.* You don't want to miss this.

KAREN FRIDAY
Speaker, author, blogger, and women's ministry leader

I have done many studies on the *I Am* statements, but Becky Harling brings fresh insights that will transform not only how you see the *Great I Am* but how you see yourself, how He sees you, and how you are called to relate to the world around you.

CHERI COWELL
Author of the *One Story, One Mission, One God* Bible study

Who Do You Say That I AM? is a wonderful study taking women into the Scriptures to get to know the real Jesus. It is well worth your time! You will never know who you are until you know who He is.

JULI SLATTERY
Psychologist and cofounder of Authentic Intimacy

People have preached, shared, discussed, debated, and tried to articulate exactly WHO Jesus is. But, do you know? Becky Harling's study will introduce you to the *I Am* statements in the Gospels and to Jesus Himself. You will be drawn into a richer, deeper, and authentic faith that will stand the test of time and circumstances.

JENNIE AFMAN DIMKOFF
International speaker and author of *Passionate Faith* and *Miracle on Hope Hill*

WHO DO YOU SAY THAT *I AM?*

A FRESH ENCOUNTER FOR DEEPER FAITH

—

BECKY HARLING

MOODY PUBLISHERS
CHICAGO

Published in association with the literary agency of The Blythe Daniel Agency, Inc., P.O. Box 64197, Colorado Springs, Colorado 80962-4197.

Edited by Amanda Cleary Eastep
Interior design: Erik M. Peterson
Author photo: Tyler Hamlet
Cover design: Dean Renninger
Cover image abstract watercolor copyright © 2017 by vetre / Shutterstock (525293773). All rights reserved.
Cover image abstract watercolor texture copyright © 2017 by solarbird / Shutterstock (130464038). All rights reserved

Library of Congress Cataloging-in-Publication Data

Names: Harling, Becky, 1957- author.
Title: Who do you say that I am? : a fresh encounter for deeper faith / Becky
    Harling.
Description: Chicago : Moody Publishers, 2018. | Includes bibliographical
    references.
Identifiers: LCCN 2017046993 (print) | LCCN 2017054891 (ebook) | ISBN
    9780802495433 | ISBN 9780802415509
Subjects: LCSH: Jesus Christ--Person and offices--Textbooks. | Bible.
    Gospels--Textbooks. | Christian women--Religious life--Textbooks.
Classification: LCC BT207 (ebook) | LCC BT207 .H37 2018 (print) | DDC
    232--dc23
LC record available at https://lccn.loc.gov/2017046993

ISBN: 978-0-8024-1550-9

All websites and phone numbers listed herein are accurate at the time of publication but may change in the future or cease to exist. The listing of website references and resources does not imply publisher endorsement of the site's entire contents. Groups and organizations are listed for informational purposes, and listing does not imply publisher endorsement of their activities.

We hope you enjoy this book from Moody Publishers. Our goal is to provide high-quality, thought-provoking books and products that connect truth to your real needs and challenges. For more information on other books and products written and produced from a biblical perspective, go to www.moodypublishers.com or write to:

Moody Publishers
820 N. LaSalle Boulevard
Chicago, IL 60610

1 3 5 7 9 10 8 6 4 2

Printed in the United States of America

This Bible study is dedicated to my precious and beautiful daughter, Stefanie Holder.
Stef, since the time you were a little girl you have been passionate about God's Word.
I've watched you study, memorize, and cling to Scripture even in the most difficult seasons of your life.
You are an incredible Bible teacher, and I love watching that unfold.
I love you!

CONTENTS

Answering the I AM   *9*

What You Can Expect from This Study   *14*

WEEK ONE   *17*
Who do you say that I am? Matthew 16:15
I Am He. John 4:26

WEEK TWO   *55*
Do you still not understand? Mark 8:17–18
I Am the Bread of Life. John 6:35

WEEK THREE   *89*
Why are you so afraid? Matthew 8:26, Mark 4:40
I Am the Good Shepherd. John 10:11

WEEK FOUR   *123*
What do you want me to do for you? Mark 10:51
I Am the Light. John 8:12

WEEK FIVE   *157*
Do you believe I am able to do this? Matthew 9:28
I Am the Resurrection and the Life. John 11:25

WEEK SIX   *193*
Do you want to get well? John 5:6
I Am the Way, the Truth, and the Life. John 14:6

WEEK SEVEN   *223*
Can you add to your life by worrying? Matthew 6:27, Luke 12:25
I Am the Vine. John 15:5

WEEK EIGHT   *257*
Has no one returned to give praise to God? Luke 17:18
I Am the Living One—The First and The Last. Revelation 1:17

Notes   *288*

Acknowledgments   *290*

ANSWERING THE *I AM*

I lay on the family room floor with my Bible open and praise music playing as I prayed, "Lord Jesus, show me who you really are! I feel like I don't know you anymore. My life feels like it's falling apart, and I'm not sure what I believe anymore!"

It was a crisis of faith. Ever had one? I had asked Jesus to be my Savior as a little girl. I grew up loving Him. As an adult, I served Him. But a series of traumatic events, including cancer, sexual abuse memories, a major move across the country, and the loss of my husband's job left me with doubts. Not just a few. Many.

Where was this Jesus I said I served? Why couldn't I feel Him? Who was He anyway, and why wasn't He behaving like the God I used to know?

Here's the thing: the chaos of life tests the strength of our spiritual levees. Do you remember Hurricane Katrina in 2005? The wicked winds and storm surge tested the strength of the levees in New Orleans, and the levees cracked under pressure. As a result, lives were lost, and New Orleans suffered billions of dollars in damage.

The chaos and trauma in my life had tested my spiritual "levees," and my faith was buckling under pressure. My questions sent me on a desperate quest. I needed deeper faith, but it had to be authentic. I was tired of pious platitudes! Real answers were crucial. As I thought through a plan, I decided I would throw out my preconceived ideas and start over by reading through the four gospels of Matthew, Mark, Luke, and John with fresh eyes and an unbiased mind to discover once again the truth of who Jesus is.

As I read and reread these books, one of my first realizations was that Jesus asked profound questions. Somehow in all my reading of the Gospels before I had missed that! These were not questions that could be answered easily with pat or simplistic answers. No, they were questions that required a person to think, analyze the evidence, and at times dig deep into Scripture—and within themselves—for the answers.

Jesus asked one of His most profound questions while He and His disciples were walking through Caesarea Philippi. Caesarea Philippi had been greatly influenced by Greek and Roman culture, and as a result, most people worshiped the Greek gods and primarily the Greek god Pan. As Jesus and His disciples walked through town, Jesus asked, "Who do people say the Son of Man is?" (Matt. 16:13).

Earlier, the Pharisees and Sadducees had challenged Jesus and asked Him for a sign to prove that He had the authority to heal the sick, cast out demons, teach in the temple, and call Himself the Son of God. The Pharisees and the Sadducees didn't recognize Jesus for who He was in spite of all their religious training in the Old Testament prophecies.

After leaving the religious leaders, Jesus and His disciples entered the city of Caesarea Philippi, where there was more false teaching. This time it was the false teaching of the Romans and Greeks who believed in a host of gods. It was in this setting that Jesus asked about the word on the street concerning His identity. The disciples answered that some thought Jesus was John the Baptist and others thought He was a prophet.

If you were to ask that same question today, I think you would receive similar answers. Some agree that Jesus was a great teacher. Many feel He was a profound historical figure, and others think He might have been a prophet. But the crux of the matter is, who do *you* say He is? After Jesus asked what others thought of Him, He then narrowed the question and pointed it at the disciples:

"Who do *you* say that I am?" (Matt. 16:15 ESV).

In response, Peter declared in triumphant faith, "You are the Messiah, the Son of the living God."

Just as Peter answered Jesus' question, you must answer His question as well. How you answer shapes the trajectory of your life.

- Was He a great prophet?
- Was He simply a profound teacher?
- Was He a political figure?
- Was He one of many ways to peace with God the Father?
- Or was He who He said He was—the great I Am, God Himself?

Or perhaps you are solid in your faith that Jesus Christ is the Son of God, the Savior of the world, but you are struggling to believe He is faithful and good because of the trials you are facing in your life right now.

Or you may be closer to Jesus than you have ever been, but you are curious about the questions He asked in the Gospels and want to know more about the *I Am* statements He made.

I wrote this Bible study for those of you who want to know, love, and trust Jesus more deeply—and for those of you who have questions about who Jesus really is and are asking, "Is He really who He says He is?"

Our culture, and even many of our churches, are confused about the identity and sufficiency of Jesus Christ. If you've experienced a crisis of faith you might be confused as well. Many in our culture believe that everyone eventually arrives at peace with God, so it really doesn't matter what you decide about Jesus. Others say, "Jesus works for me, just find what works for you!"

The decision you reach about who Jesus is will be the most profound decision of your life, and it has extreme ramifications. But I'm getting ahead of myself. For now, I want to challenge you to enter this Bible study with an open mind and heart. Take a look at the questions Jesus asked and examine the claims Jesus made about Himself. Look at the evidence, and then answer, "Who do *I* say He is?"

Nothing describes Jesus' identity as profoundly as His *I Am* statements. In my journey toward deeper faith, I began to study the *I Am* statements as the answer to the questions Jesus was asking. As I studied, I fell head over heels in love with Jesus all over again!

The more I discovered, the more I wanted to know. A little bit of Jesus was not enough. I wanted all of Him, and I wanted Him to have all of me. My life circumstances didn't change, but I sure did. I became confident in Christ. My doubts settled down. My fears quieted, and my faith flourished.

Friend, this study is the result of those years when I buried myself in the Gospels, answered His questions personally, and deepened the roots of my faith.

Maybe you're just wondering. What is so intriguing about Jesus Christ anyway? Why bother answering the questions He asked? Maybe it has felt to you that Christians are judgmental. What makes them think they have the corner on truth?

Maybe you are a believer who is struggling to believe He is really who He says He is. Or maybe you aren't experiencing a crisis of faith, and you are excited to hear His answers and understand Him in a new way.

Do you want to deepen and strengthen your faith so that when the winds of chaos blow, you stand steady and strong? Come with me on a journey—a journey to discover the claims that Jesus made about Himself and how those claims can change your life.

Jesus' questions are worthy of your consideration. If He is God as He says He is, then you, like me, need a divine encounter with Him, an encounter that revitalizes your faith and transforms your life!

But first, let me warn you. When we come face to face with Christ, He invites us to an exciting adventure. It may rock our world and shake us to the core, but it's worth it because there is no one like Jesus. He is the Lord of the universe, the great "I Am."

So are you in? Are you up for an exciting and life-changing encounter?

Think about it:

What if you could walk away from this study with deeper faith that Jesus is exactly who He said He was?

What if the next time a crisis hits your life, your faith is strong and rock solid?

What if you decided to follow Jesus and passionately live your life for Him? How would your life be different?

WHAT YOU CAN EXPECT FROM THIS STUDY

As you begin this journey to answer Jesus' questions and consider His *I Am* statements, I want you to know how excited I am for you. Whenever I start a new adventure, I like to know what to expect. I bet you feel similarly.

Each week will begin with a question Jesus asked. We'll examine the passage where He asked the question and the setting of the question, then we'll move to an *I Am* statement that answers that question.

Each week you'll have five days of homework. I can hear you groaning. Homework? Don't worry. The homework is simply a guide to help you delve more deeply into Scripture and discover the wonder of each statement. If you miss a day, don't panic. Simply catch up as you go through the study. Similarly, if a day's homework impacts you deeply, and you feel you need another day to absorb that particular truth, take the extra time. Make the workbook work for you!

Each day's homework will include a short passage or several short passages of Scripture to help you gain a deeper understanding of the truth behind Jesus' identity, as well as several questions for you to answer. Some of the questions will be inductive in nature and some will be reflective. Before you begin each day's homework, pause, pray, and ask the Holy Spirit to help you absorb the truth you are studying.

Each week, your workbook will include the following sections:

• **EXPLORE** This section will include a guided study of the passage or passages of Scripture related to an *I Am* statement made by Jesus.

You'll have the opportunity to peruse Scripture and answer questions to help you explore the statement further. You'll notice that throughout the study there will be references to words in their original language. Next to these words you'll see (Strong's #_____) with a specific number. *Strong's Exhaustive Concordance* is a very accessible tool to help you understand the meaning behind words used in the Bible. It's a great idea for you to become acquainted with this concordance and comfortable using it as a resource for diving deeper into a passage. Whenever you see a word with a reference to Strong's after it, look the word up online and check it out.

- **REFLECT** In this section you'll answer a few questions designed for reflection on your own personal growth. There are no right or wrong answers in this section, so be honest with yourself. This section is designed to help you process what you're experiencing.

- **MEMORIZE** Most weeks there will be a suggested passage of Scripture for you to memorize. Memorizing increases the Holy Spirit's vocabulary in our lives and cements His truth in our hearts.

- **PRAISE** Each day I'll encourage you to praise Christ for some element of His character. Many days, I'll include a song for you to listen to in order to prompt your praise. Scripture teaches us that God inhabits the praises of His people. As we become intentional about praising God each day, I believe our faith grows deeper.

I'm praying for you as we journey through this Bible study together. Let's get started!

Becky Harling

Becky Harling

who do you say that I AM?

He said to them, "But who do you say that I am?"

MATTHEW 16:15 (ESV)

I AM HE

Then Jesus declared,
"I, the one speaking to you—I am he."

JOHN 4:26

WEEK 1 | DAY 1

WHO DO YOU SAY THAT *I AM*?

MATTHEW 16:15

> *Good questions inform; great questions transform.*
> –John Maxwell

If I were to ask you what's the most transformational question you've been asked, how would you answer?

- Will you marry me?
- What do you want out of your life?
- Do you want this job?
- Do you want to have a baby?
- Do you want to move across the country?
- Do you want to buy a house?

If you had asked Jesus' disciples about the most transformational question they had been asked, their minds likely would have traveled back to a conversation they had had with Jesus while walking through Caesarea Philippi. The conversation began with the question Jesus asked about what others thought of Him and ended with Jesus asking the most pivotal question the disciples had been asked,

Who do you say that *I Am*?

EXPLORE

Read Matthew 16:13–20. Write your observations.

Write out Jesus' question to the disciples in the space below, and then circle the phrase "I am."

In order to understand how important that phrase "I am" is, let's take a look at the first time God introduced Himself as *I Am*.

Read Exodus 3:1–14.

Centuries before Christ, Moses was stuck out in the Midian Desert taking care of his father-in-law's sheep. Moses had discovered that though he was raised by Pharaoh's daughter, his birth mom was an Israelite slave who had lived in bondage in Egypt. Seeing God's people suffer such great oppression, Moses felt irate, and in a moment of pure rage, killed an Egyptian taskmaster. Knowing he could face death, Moses fled to the desert, married, and took care of his father-in-law's sheep. But the questions that rattled in his mind over the plight of God's people tortured him. Talk about a crisis of faith. Moses definitely had one!

There in the wilderness, wrestling with great questions of faith, Moses encountered a burning bush. The intriguing thing about the bush was that though it was on fire, it was not being consumed.

Describe Moses's reaction to the burning bush.

God spoke to Moses from the burning bush and gave him instructions. Describe the instructions God gave to Moses.

How did God introduce Himself to Moses in Exodus 3:6?

Read Exodus 3:13–14. How did God respond when Moses asked, "What should I say to the Israelites when they ask your name?"

Every Jewish child growing up at the time of Jesus would have heard this story. So when Jesus asked the disciples, "But who do you say that I am?" (Matt. 16:15 ESV), what was the implication?

JOHN'S RECORD OF THE *I AM* STATEMENTS OF JESUS

One of Jesus' best friends recorded His *I Am* statements. His name was John, and he would have been with Jesus when Jesus asked, "But who do you say that I am?" (Matt. 16:15 ESV). He was one of the disciples and identified himself often throughout his writings as "the disciple whom Jesus loved" (John 13:23). Many biblical scholars believe he was Jesus' best earthly friend.

But, he didn't start out that way. When Jesus first met John, He nicknamed him (and his brother James) "Son of Thunder." John was a hothead who easily exploded.

One time when Jesus was criticized by some Samaritans, John wanted Jesus to call down fire from heaven to destroy the whole town (Luke 9:52–56). Jesus explained to John that vengeance wasn't the way He did things.

Not only did John lose his temper, but he was also a bit self-centered and arrogant. In one instance, he asked Jesus to do for him whatever he asked because he wanted a seat of prominence, power, and authority in Christ's kingdom. The other followers of Jesus who overheard this conversation were not very happy about John's request (Mark 10:35–44). Hotheaded, arrogant, craving power and authority—not exactly the type you'd imagine Jesus being best friends with, right?

But as Jesus loved, accepted, affirmed, and challenged John, he changed. Being with Jesus completely transformed him. John was an eyewitness to the miracles of Jesus and was the only one of His friends standing at the foot of the cross when Jesus died.

John was one of the first people to witness the resurrected Christ and eventually became one of the founding leaders of the early church. He authored the gospel of John; 1, 2, and 3 John; and the book of Revelation. His relationship with Jesus was transformational.

When John wrote his gospel, he said his desired intent was for his readers to believe that Jesus was exactly who He said He was, the great I Am. ". . . but these are written so that you may believe that Jesus is the Christ, the Son of God, and that by believing you may have life in his name" (John 20:31 ESV).

John is the only gospel writer who recorded all of Jesus' *I Am* statements.

To give you an overview of the *I Am* statements of Jesus that we'll be considering throughout this study, look up the following verses and write the *I Am* statement next to each one.

THE *I AM* STATEMENTS OF JESUS

John 4:26

John 6:35

John 8:12

John 10:11

John 11:25

John 14:6

John 15:1

Revelation 1:17

Let's return to the scene where Jesus was asking the disciples about His identity.

Read Matthew 16:15–16. Notice Peter's response to Jesus Christ's question and write it in the space below.

The Greek word for Christ that's used here is from the Hebrew word meaning Messiah. Peter was acknowledging that Jesus Christ was the promised Messiah. Keep that in mind for tomorrow when we'll look at another person who recognized Jesus as the promised Messiah!

REFLECT

In your life, have you ever had a crisis of faith? If so, describe that crisis below.

How can a crisis of faith be transformed into a catalyst for deeper faith?

What are you hoping for out of this study?

MEMORIZE

This week, memorize Romans 8:1–2.

PRAISE

Listen to the worship song "I Am" by Influence Music & Melody Noel featuring William Matthews. As you listen—even if you are in a season of doubt—intentionally praise God that He is the great I Am. Praise awakens deeper faith in our hearts.

IN NEED OF A MESSIAH

If there is anything that can create a crisis of faith, it's guilt! Often when someone feels guilty, they back up from God rather than run toward God. In their prison of shame they cry out, "Why would God want me? He can't forgive me; I'm such a mess!"

This was the case for Jade. After experiencing the horror of rape, Jade entered the porn industry. Because she felt God hadn't protected her, she thought—why not give up and enter an industry where she could make money with her body? When a friend invited her to come to God, Jade's response spoke volumes about the shame she felt: "Why would He want me now?"

The irony is that Jesus *always* pursues the sinner! In Jade's case, God continually placed concerned Christians in her path who loved her and prayed for her. Eventually, Jade found the courage to come to Jesus and allow Him to cleanse her shame with His living water. Jade now speaks all over the country helping others to find Jesus.

Jesus once had a conversation with a woman who, like Jade, had a shameful history and desperately needed a Messiah.

Who do you say that I Am?
I Am He

EXPLORE

Read John 4:1–26. Write your observations in the space below.

I believe that Jesus' choice to travel through Samaria was intentional. Many Jews avoided the region of Samaria like the plague. To help you understand why the Jews and Samaritans hated each other, here's a little history.

Under Solomon's son Rehoboam, Israel split in two (1 Kings 12). The northern part of Israel was led by Jeroboam, and the southern part of Israel, which was called Judah, was ruled by Rehoboam. Jeroboam was afraid that the two kingdoms would once again unite and that he would not be the new king of the northern kingdom, so he established his own pagan religion rather than encouraging his people to worship Jehovah. He constructed two golden calves and told his people to worship those (1 Kings 12:25–33). (Steve and I recently visited that exact spot in Israel. What a reminder to never let idolatry in any form into our lives!)

Later, a wicked king named Omri built the city of Samaria, which became synonymous with the entire northern kingdom. He also built a temple and created an altar to Baal (1 Kings 16:24–34).

When the Assyrians defeated Israel, many Israelites intermarried with the heathen nations, resulting in a nation of mixed races and pagan beliefs (2 Kings 17:23). Israel's religion intermingled with idolatry, and the Samaritans developed their own kind of religion. Although they professed to believe in the God of Israel and the coming Messiah (see John 4:25), they accepted only the first five books of the Law and rejected the rest of the Old Testament.[1]

I love that Jesus stepped past cultural norms and racial prejudice to seek out the Samaritan woman. In a culture that devalued women, Jesus makes His first *I Am* statement to a woman! While religious systems often devalue women, Jesus honors women.

It was noon when Jesus sat by the well. Most women traveled to the well in groups early in the morning or late in the evening in order to avoid heat, but the Samaritan woman made the trek alone in the heat of the day.

Read John 4:6. Why do you think the Samaritan woman came in the heat of the day to draw water?

Read John 4:7–9. Describe the woman's attitude when Jesus asked her for a drink of water.

Read John 4:10–14. What is the meaning behind the "living water" that Jesus spoke of?

Read John 4:15–18. How did Jesus respond when the woman asked for living water?

Read John 4:19–20. Describe the Samaritan woman's response to Jesus.

Read John 4:21–24. How did Jesus describe true worship?

What do you think it means to worship in spirit and in truth?

Read John 4:25–26. When the woman said she knew the Messiah was coming, how did Jesus respond? Write His *I Am* statement here:

REFLECT

Are there people groups you feel prejudice toward? How does your prejudice manifest?

If you were to describe "living water" to a friend, how would you describe it?

When someone confronts you with a fault, how do you usually respond?

What generally triggers your guilt? Thoughts about your past, your present, or your relationships?

Write out Romans 8:1–2. What does it mean to you to be "in Christ"?

PRAISE

Listen to "Into the Deep" by Citipointe Live. As you listen, praise God that His living water is always available and accessible.

WEEK 1 | DAY 3

THE MESSIAH WHO TAKES AWAY YOUR GUILT

The Samaritan woman said she knew the Messiah would come. The word *messiah* in the Greek literally means, "anointed one" (Strong's #3323).[2] As the Messiah, Jesus came as the anointed one to heal our guilt and shame.

The truth is, we are all guilty because none of us are perfect (Rom. 3:23). Our guilt separates us from God, and according to God's Word, sin must be punished. The great news is that as the Messiah, Jesus came and took the punishment by dying on the cross so that we wouldn't have to be punished for our sin. He offers us forgiveness and freedom from shame.

When we receive Christ's forgiveness, we are forever set free from guilt and shame. However, we often still ask the question: "Why do I still feel guilty?" Today, let's talk about guilt, conviction, and repentance.

EXPLORE

Read Romans 3:23. What does this Scripture teach you about sin?

Read Romans 6:23. According to this verse, what is the penalty for sin?

Read John 3:16. How did God take care of this problem for us?

Read James 2:10. Write your own personal definition of guilt. According to this passage, why do you personally need a Messiah?

THE DIFFERENCE BETWEEN GUILT AND CONVICTION

Guilt felt before repentance is the conviction of the Holy Spirit, but guilt felt after repentance is condemnation and does not come from God. After we have received Jesus Christ as our Savior, condemnation is *never* God's plan for us. Conviction about sin as a believer *is* part of His plan, because God's primary goal in our lives is to transform us into the image of Jesus.

Read Romans 8:1–2. Write it out in the space below.

What do these verses teach you about being set free from guilt?

Read John 16:8.

The Holy Spirit convicts us of sin. The word "convict" is a translation of the Greek word *elencho*, which means "to convince someone of the truth."[3]

When the Holy Spirit convicts us of sin, we come to realize the truth about our wrongdoing, and we experience godly sorrow that leads to repentance. We turn from our sin and move toward obedience to God's commands.

When the Spirit of God brings conviction, we can respond in
several ways:

- Defensiveness
- Denial
- Regret that we got caught
- Godly sorrow
- Diverting attention from our sinfulness
- Shame and depression

Read John 4:16–20. Which of the responses listed above do you see
in how the Samaritan woman responded to Jesus?

Which of those responses is most often the way you respond?

Read 2 Corinthians 7:10. Describe godly sorrow in your own words.

Read 1 John 1:9.

The word for confess in this verse carries the idea of "agreeing with." When we confess our sins, we agree with God that what we've done is wrong. It's the idea behind the ability to say, "I was wrong."

According to this verse, what happens when we agree with God that what we've done is wrong?

REFLECT

Is it hard for you to say, "I was wrong"? If so, how do you most often respond when someone points out wrongdoing in your life?

Is there an area of your life where the Spirit of God has convicted you recently? Conviction prompts confession. Write a prayer of confession below about the area where the Holy Spirit has most recently convicted you.

PRAISE

Listen to "Lord You Know" by Riana Nel. As you listen, thank Jesus that though He knows everything you've ever done, He loves you deeply and died for you!

WEEK 1 | DAY 4

HOW TO SHUT UP THE ACCUSER

I felt upset, confused, and angry. I was in California getting ready to speak at a women's conference but had just received an extremely critical email. The person writing the email had lashed out with many accusations over the fact that I was sharing my story. My head was spinning. I felt Satan hurling every insult and accusation at me as I closed my computer. His messages went something like this, "You're emotionally unstable! You shouldn't be out there speaking and at the very least not telling your story. You're unfit to speak."

I cried, "Lord, how can I speak tomorrow? I've got nothing!" Instantly, the Holy Spirit reminded me of how to shut up Satan. I turned on some praise music and grabbed my Bible. Thankfully, no one was home in the house where I was staying. I began praising God and quoting Scripture.

If anyone had been looking through the window, they would have thought I was nuts! There I was, with praise music blaring, marching around the house with my Bible in hand praising my way through the alphabet at the top of my lungs. . .

"Lord, I praise you because you have all authority, and Satan can't thwart your plans! I praise you because you're the Blessed Controller of all things. I praise you because you promise to deliver me from evil, and God, this feels evil. I praise you that you're in control!"

I continued until I literally felt a breakthrough. I finally relaxed, praised God that He would speak the next day, and took some time to rest.

Here's what I know: Even though a person has received Christ as her Messiah and asked for forgiveness of sins, Satan will try to attack with feelings of guilt and shame.

Today, we're going to take a look at shame and false guilt. And I'm going to teach you *how* to tell the enemy loud and clear to "Shut up!" Are you ready? You must learn this skill to help protect yourself from the taunts and torments of Satan.

EXPLORE

Read Revelation 12:10–11. What is Satan called in these verses?

As the accuser, Satan lives his life around one single purpose: accusing you. Sad, huh? But he loves nothing more than to get you twisted into fits of self-doubt and shame so that he renders you useless at proclaiming what God has done in your life. How does he do this? He has several strategies, and here are just a few:

Guilt over sin you've already confessed. I've seen this strategy employed time after time as I've spoken at women's conferences, particularly in the realm of sexuality and abortion. Friend, may I speak directly to you? No matter what you've done, no matter how horrible the act, if you've confessed your sin, Christ has forgiven you. God no longer dwells on your sin, so neither should you! When Satan hurls accusations at you, you must stand tall and slap him with Scripture! You might say, "Satan, shut up! In the name and power of Jesus Christ, you have no place here. I'm under the authority of Jesus Christ. My sin has been covered by the blood of the Lamb. I've confessed my sin, and Jesus has been faithful and just to forgive my sin and to cleanse me completely (1 John 1:9). I am chosen, holy, and dearly loved" (Col. 3:12).

Read Psalm 103:12. What does this verse teach us about God removing our sin from us?

Guilt over unmet or unrealistic expectations. No matter how hard you try, you will not keep everyone happy. Some people will have expectations of you that you simply cannot live up to. When you disappoint them, they manipulate you, and you end up feeling guilty. Here are a few examples:

- Your schedule is very busy right now. Time is at a premium, and you're trying to prioritize your husband and children. A friend feels hurt because you haven't spent enough time with her. You feel guilty because you're afraid you're not being a good friend.

- Your definition of being a "good mother" means always baking homemade cookies like your neighbor, but you hate baking, and every time you try, you burn the cookies. When you see what's packed in your neighbor's kids' lunch boxes, you feel guilty.

- Your mother feels you need to prioritize spending time with her over the Bible study you're attending at your church. She brings it up every week informing you that she's getting old, and if you were a "good Christian," you would spend time with her instead. You hang up the phone as feelings of guilt wash over you.

What you'll notice about each of those examples is that none of them contradict a biblical principle. False guilt has nothing to do with truth or what the Word of God says is sin. False guilt often challenges our personal boundaries. But it's godly to set boundaries.

Read Mark 1:35–39. What does this story about Jesus teach you about setting boundaries?

Guilt over evil done to you. As a child, I was sexually abused. Evil was done to me. As an adult, I struggled with a pervasive sense of being unclean. What I was struggling with was a profound sense of shame. I felt guilty and embarrassed about what had been done to me. As a result of the shame I felt, I took on guilt that was not my own. It wasn't until I worked with a counselor and pursued Christ as my Healer that God set me free from shame.

Read Ezekiel 18:20. What does this verse teach you about taking responsibility for another person's sin?

How does this verse release you from shame about evil committed against you?

When you feel guilty, ask yourself the following questions:

- Have I disobeyed God in some area of my life?
- Is Satan bringing up my past and something that I've already confessed?
- Am I feeling guilty because I don't measure up to someone's expectations for me?
- Am I feeling guilty because of evil done against me?

If your answer is yes to the first question, become a fast confessor. Turn from your sin, and get on board with God's desires for you. If it's any of the other three, remind yourself that you are holy and blameless.

REFLECT

The two best weapons I know for fighting Satan when he tries to throw guilt and shame at you are: Praise and Scripture.

Read Psalm 149:6. Write this verse in the space below.

CREATE AN EMERGENCY FAITH KIT

Many homes have an emergency kit for when family members get hurt or need first aid. Similarly in our spiritual walks, we need an emergency kit of Scripture verses and praise songs that we can go to instinctively when Satan is attacking or we're facing a crisis.

In the space below, write out five verses of your choice that you will keep in your emergency kit, and write down the name of five praise songs that you will either sing or play when Satan starts with his "blah, blah, blah." I will get you started with the first Scripture verse, and the rest you can choose on your own.

> **Scripture Verses**
>
> 1. Philippians 2:9–11. "Therefore God exalted him to the highest place and gave him the name that is above every name, that at the name of Jesus every knee should bow, in heaven and on earth and under the earth, and every tongue acknowledge that Jesus is Lord, to the glory of God the Father."

2.

3.

4.

5.

Praise Songs

1.

2.

3.

4.

5.

MEMORIZE

Review Romans 8:1. Write it out on an index card, and tape the card where you will see it often.

PRAISE

In the space below, write out a prayer of praise thanking Jesus that He is the victor over Satan.

Listen to "Blameless" by Dara Maclean. As you listen, praise God that He came as the Messiah to offer you freedom from guilt and shame and that He calls you blameless, holy, and chosen!

CHANGED!

The life of the Samaritan woman was forever changed when she met Jesus. In fact, Scripture tells us she went and told all her friends to come meet the man who had told her everything she had ever done. As a result of her encounter with Jesus, many other Samaritans came to faith in Him as their Messiah.

Read John 4:27–42. As you read, write your observations in the space below.

Read John 4:27. Why do you think the disciples were surprised that Jesus was talking to a woman?

Read John 4:28–29. Circle the word "leaving" in the passage.

When we meet Jesus and recognize Him as our Messiah, we leave behind our old way of thinking and doing things. The apostle Paul wrote in 2 Corinthians 5:17, "Therefore, if anyone is in Christ, the new creation has come: The old has gone, the new is here!" When someone puts her faith and trust in Jesus Christ, everything changes, and she now has a new life agenda—God's agenda!

EXPLORE

How is this illustrated by the Samaritan woman in John 4:29–30?

Read John 4:35. Circle the phrase "open your eyes."

What do you think Jesus meant when He said the fields were ripe and ready for harvest?

How do you think it might help you to "open your eyes" to see the people who are ready to hear about Jesus?

Read John 4:39–42. What was the response from the people in town to the Samaritan woman's story?

Read John 4:42. Once the people from town heard Jesus, what did they believe about Him?

REFLECT

The Samaritan woman's life changed drastically after she met Jesus.

How has your life changed since you put your faith and trust in Jesus?

As soon as the Samaritan woman met Jesus, she wanted to bring her friends to introduce them to Him. She simply told them her story. When was the last time you told one of your friends about Jesus?

Think about the highlights of your story. In the space below write down 4–5 bullet points of your story that you could use to tell other people about Jesus.

As you reflect back on this week, what principle has stuck out to you most as far as dumping your bucket of guilt?

What is one action step you will take as a result of this week's study?

MEMORIZE

Review Romans 8:1–2.

PRAISE

That God would send His own Son to take the punishment for our sin is nothing short of incredible grace. As we close out this week, listen to "How Can It Be" by Lauren Daigle. As you listen, praise God for His incredible grace and forgiveness. You are free from guilt and shame. Celebrate!

do you still not understand?

Aware of their discussion, Jesus asked them: "Why are you talking about having no bread? Do you still not see or understand? Are your hearts hardened? Do you have eyes but fail to see, and ears but fail to hear? And don't you remember?"

MARK 8:17–18

I AM THE BREAD OF LIFE

Then Jesus declared, "I am the bread of life. Whoever comes to me will never go hungry, and whoever believes in me will never be thirsty."

JOHN 6:35

WEEK 2 | DAY 1

DO YOU STILL NOT UNDERSTAND?

Mark 8:17–18

> *This is where we find the kind of love we most deeply need—*
> *not in human relationships, but in God.*
> *If we want real love, ideal love, perfect love,*
> *God's heart is where to find it.*
> *It's the only love big enough to meet the God-sized needs*
> *of your life and mine.*
> —Ruth Myers

Known for provocative questions and powerful miracles, Jesus drew people like a magnet. This week we're going to look at Jesus' question,

Do you still not understand?

In order to understand Jesus' question, we must first explore two of His miracles.

The rich, the poor, the messy, and the marginalized all came flocking to Jesus. They had heard about how He had turned the water into wine (John 2), healed the Roman centurion's servant (Matt. 8:5–13; Luke 7:1–10), raised the widow's son (Luke 7:11–17), calmed the storm (Matt. 8:23–27; Mark 4:35–41; Luke 8:22–25), and cast out demons into a herd of pigs (Matt. 8:28–34; Mark 5:1–20; Luke 8:26–39).

Sometime after these miracles, Jesus sat on a grassy hillside enjoying the quiet breeze and a moment with His friends. The peace was soon disrupted by a mob scrambling up the hillside in frantic search of Him. A large crowd once again gathered to hear Him. Not hundreds. Thousands. Thousands of needy and desperate people longing to catch a glimpse of His next miracle or receive one for themselves.

There were likely 10,000 people there! We read about the scene in all four of the gospel accounts (Matt. 14:13–21; Mark 6:30–44; Luke 9:10–17), but it's John's account we're going to focus on.

EXPLORE

Read John 6:1–14. Imagine you were there with Jesus and the disciples.

What did it feel like for you to see a mob of thousands climbing up the hill to see Jesus?

How would you describe what you saw to a friend?

There doesn't seem to be any panic on Jesus' part. How would you describe His mood when He asked Philip, "Where shall we buy food for these people to eat?" (John 6:5–6).

John tells us that Jesus was testing Philip to strengthen His faith. Jesus knew the miracle He was about to perform, but He wanted to test Philip. The Greek word for test is *peirazo*. It means a proving experience. Jesus wasn't setting Philip up for failure. He was setting the stage to demonstrate to Philip the enormity of His ability to meet the vastness of our human need.

Meanwhile, Andrew, another one of Jesus' disciples, pointed out that a little boy in the crowd had made his lunch available (John 6:8–9). Don't you wonder what was going through Philip's mind when Andrew mentioned the little boy's lunch to Jesus?

Do you think Andrew genuinely believed that Jesus could meet the needs of the crowd by using a small boy's lunch? Or do you think he was being sarcastic? Why or why not?

What evidence do you have to support your view?

The little boy's lunch included five small barley loaves of bread and two small fish. Barley loaves indicated that his family was likely poor. Only the poorest in society used barley to bake bread. I have several little grandsons. None of them are poor. May I just say, it's really hard for hungry little boys to share their lunch? Kudos to this little guy for his willing heart! Not only was he likely hungry, but it's also possible he often had to go without because his parents couldn't afford more food, yet he was willing to share!

Jesus loves kids, and I'm sure it put a huge smile on the Almighty's face that this little boy had the faith to believe that He could take his tiny lunch and share it with thousands. Imagine the story the little boy told his mama when he got home!

Jesus instructed the crowd to sit down, and then He offered thanks and began tearing off pieces of bread and fish. Miraculously there was more than enough for everyone. Can you imagine the eyes of the little boy who shared his lunch with Jesus? I bet they were popped wide open. And there were even leftovers. It's so like Jesus to provide more than enough, isn't it?

The second miracle Jesus performed was very similar and is found in the gospel of Mark.

Read Mark 8:1–10. How is the feeding of the 4,000 similar to the feeding of the 5,000?

What do both the feeding of the 5,000 and the feeding of the 4,000 teach you about the magnitude of Christ's love for people?

After the miracles, Jesus left the region and traveled across the Sea of Galilee to the region of Dalmanutha. When they arrived, rather than celebrating the compassionate loving heart of Christ in feeding the multitudes, the Pharisees greeted Jesus with a skeptical spirit and began demanding a sign from Him to prove He really was from God.

Later, Jesus warned the disciples to be careful of the "yeast of the Pharisees." Jesus was cautioning His disciples about a spirit of skepticism that might block their full experience of Christ's love and provision. But the disciples missed the point. They thought Jesus was rebuking them for forgetting to bring bread. Nothing could have been further from the truth.

Jesus wanted them to understand fully that He Himself was God's provision for every need. He had just fed 5,000 people, then turned around and miraculously fed another 4,000. Did He really need the disciples to remember to bring bread? Hardly! It was in this context that Jesus asked His disciples, "Do you still not understand?" (Mark 8:21).

REFLECT

As you consider Jesus' question, what do you think He wanted His disciples to understand?

Read John 6:15. What did the crowd perceive to be their greatest need after the feeding of the 5,000?

Read Mark 8:11. What did the Pharisees perceive to be their greatest need after the feeding of the 4,000?

Often, when we feel needy, we draw an incorrect conclusion and run to the wrong source to fill our need. We're similar to the crowds that followed Jesus. We believe a new political system will solve our problems. We beg God for a miracle in our marriage believing that if our marriage just changed we'd feel deeply loved and the ache in our soul would diminish. Or if God would only allow us to have a baby, the twinge of incompleteness would be healed. We crave and chase anything that we believe will fill the longing in our souls. And to make matters worse, when the throbbing doesn't go away, we anesthetize our pain with social media, food, alcohol, shopping, or drugs.

When you feel bored, lonely, or disappointed with life, what do you generally run to in order to anesthetize your pain? What would it look like instead for you to run to Jesus?

MEMORIZE

Begin memorizing the following passage from Ephesians 3:17b–19:

> I pray that you, being rooted and established in love,
>
> May have power, together with all the Lord's holy people, to grasp how wide and long and high and deep is the love of Christ,
>
> And to know this love that surpasses knowledge—
>
> That you may be filled to the measure of all the fullness of God.

PRAISE

Listen to "Build My Life" by Passion featuring Brett Younker. As you listen, praise God that His love is the only sure foundation for your life!

WEEK 2 | DAY 2

HUNGRY FOR LOVE

After the crowd witnessed the extraordinary miracles of Jesus, they wanted more. Not more bread; their tummies were full! They wanted another great show. Hungry for another miracle, they went in search of Jesus and found Him on the other side of the Sea of Galilee.

I've visited Israel several times and have taken a boat across the Sea of Galilee. The lake is beautiful. It's the largest freshwater lake in Israel, and it is approximately 53 km in circumference, about 21 km long, and 13 km wide.[4] What strikes me is the determination of the crowd to travel such a long distance to find Jesus. They felt desperate. But they lacked the self-awareness to understand the root of their desperation. Let's pick up the story just after the crowd finds Jesus.

Do you still not understand?

I Am the Bread of Life

EXPLORE

Read John 6:25–40.

Jesus looked into their souls and saw the deepest need of their hearts, which were famished for His love. Instead of providing another phenomenal show of His power, Jesus cautioned them, "Do not work for food that spoils, but for food that endures to eternal life" (John 6:27).

In what ways do people work hard for food that spoils or disappoints?

What do you think Jesus was referring to when He said, "Food that endures to eternal life"?

After Jesus promised that He, the Son of Man, would give them this food, the crowd asked, "What must we do to do the works God requires?" (John 6:28). History demonstrates that people are always trying to "earn" God's approval.

Think through some of the religious systems you are familiar with. How do people in those systems try to earn God's favor?

Jesus answers the crowd with basically one word: believe. Just believe that God loves you and sent His Son Jesus to prove that love.

The word "believe" is *pisteúō* in the Greek. It means to have confidence with the sacred significance of being persuaded by the Lord (Strong's #4100). It carries the idea of being fully persuaded and having trust in a person. In other words, it goes beyond simply affirming with your mouth to relying on completely.[5] John uses the word "believe" more than any of the other gospel writers. That word is going to keep showing up throughout our study.

When Jesus said, "Believe," it was as if He was saying, "Don't just affirm that you believe with your mouth. Instead, fully rely on my unfailing love for you. Be confident that *you* are loved deeply by the Father and that He sent Me to prove His commitment to you."

REFLECT

In what ways would your life look different if you fully relied on Christ's love for you?

It is astounding when that truth finally penetrates the deepest place of your fragile, insecure heart, and you realize there is nothing you can do to earn God's love. He already loves you! Completely. Categorically. Crazily. In. Love. With. You.

Pause for a moment, breathe, and allow that truth to sink in. Even as followers of Christ, we sometimes fall back to old patterns of trying to earn God's love. We serve harder and try harder to live good Christian moral lives, but the truth is, it doesn't make God love you any more or any less. He honestly couldn't love you more than He does at this moment. How crazy is that?

Only Jesus, as the Bread of Life, is able to love you that completely. He is the only true source of satisfaction for your deepest love needs. Just to be sure we fully understand the depth of His love for us, He repeats His claim three times.

Read John 6:35–59. List the three verses where Jesus claims to be the Bread of Life. Next to each reference write out in its entirety the claim Jesus makes.

Bread was a daily staple for the people to whom Jesus spoke. The crowd listening to Jesus knew that they couldn't live without the daily sustenance of bread. Similarly, we can't live without the daily supply of His love. The greatest hunger and thirst we experience is to feel loved and accepted. As we mentioned yesterday, God designed us with a divine ache that only His perfect love can satisfy. Human love, wonderful as it is, will at some level disappoint us and let us down. It is only Christ's perfect, infinite, complete love that comes with the promise of satisfaction.

Jesus offered a guarantee: Those who come to Him for His love will *never* have to feel hungry or thirsty for love again.

If this is true, what part does human love play in filling our need for love?

Notice the emphasis on the word "life" in Jesus' claims. The word Jesus used for life here is *zóé*, a noun meaning life, both of physical (present) and of spiritual (particularly future) existence (Strong's #2222). But when He goes on to refer to Himself as the "living bread," the word for life is the present active participle of the verb *záō*, to live, to experience God's gift of life (Strong's #2198).

In other words, Jesus doesn't invite us to come to Him for life only once. His life-giving love is ongoing and active. We are never more alive than when we are being nourished by Christ's perfect love. Author Ruth Myers describes it this way: "God is our first Source, and ultimately the only Source, of all we need for a full and satisfied life."[6]

Pause and think about that truth for a second. What impact does that have for you personally to realize that Christ is ultimately your only true Source for a satisfied life? How would you describe a completely satisfied life?

According to John 6:51, how did Christ prove His love?

How have you personally responded to His demonstration of love?

MEMORIZE

Review Ephesians 3:17b–19.

PRAISE

One very effective way of writing out prayers of praise is to use Scripture. Using the Scripture we are memorizing this week (Eph. 3:17b–19), write your own prayer of praise in the space below.

Listen to "You Are Enough" by All People's Worship featuring Keri Denison (We Release).

WHAT DOES PERFECT LOVE LOOK LIKE?

Yesterday, we unpacked the *I Am* statement "I Am the Bread of Life." Honestly, for years I had difficulty feeling loved by God. Sure, I knew He loved me. After all, the Bible told me so. I taught the love of God, and I believed the Bible taught truth. I just couldn't feel it. And I wasn't sure you were supposed to *feel* it. I mean, did God want me to *feel* loved by Him or was it enough to know it in my head?

In my mind, God felt a bit cold and emotionally distant. Perhaps, aloof? It was the way I was raised. He was holy and untouchable. To visualize Him as madly in love with me felt, well—sacrilegious. He was under contractual agreement to love me, but what exactly was the nature of that love?

Whenever I tried to visualize His love, I could almost see Him rolling His Almighty eyes, heaving a great sigh, and saying, "Well, of course I love her!" But I always imagined that somewhere under the surface He groaned, "She annoys the heck out of me, but I'm God. I have to love her!"

As I began to really delve deeply into Jesus' *I Am* statements, I had a new encounter with God's love. I discovered He really *wants* me to feel deeply and categorically loved by Him! And guess what? He's actually a pretty emotional God. Think about it. He experienced the full range of emotions. He cried at Lazarus's tomb (John 11:35). He got angry in the temple and flipped a few tables (John 2:15–17). He felt deep love for His friends (John 15:13–14), and John clearly felt loved by him, because God's love is one of his favorite topics.

Today, we're going to dive into God's love more deeply. My prayer for you is that you will encounter His love with a new set of eyes, and that as you experience His love, you'll be changed.

EXPLORE

Read 1 John 3:1–3, 4:10, 4:17–18. When you read the word "lavish" in 1 John 3:1, what comes to your mind?

The word "lavish" carries the idea of going beyond the expected measure or exceeding all expectations. God is not a stingy God. He's extravagant and lavish in His love for us, going above and beyond any expectation we could possibly have.

As part of God's lavish love, He gives us everything we need for life and godliness (2 Peter 1:3).

What are some of the things needed to live a spiritually and emotionally healthy life?

According to 1 John 4:10, God is the ultimate source of "real" love. In His love, He sent Jesus for what purpose?

The phrase "atoning sacrifice" (Strong's #2434) that John used to describe Jesus has amazing significance as far as His love for us. The phrase is used to describe Christ and His sacrificial death to satisfy the wrath of God against sin. It also gives us a picture of Christ providing a cover for us so that when God the Father looks at us, we look as holy to Him as Jesus! Through Christ's atoning sacrifice, God offers us mercy, grace, and freedom from fear.

1 John 4:18 teaches us that perfect love, like what we have in Christ, banishes every fear. What are some specific fears that you can let go of because of Christ's atoning sacrifice?

The prophet Zephaniah paints a beautiful picture of God's deep love.

Read Zephaniah 3:17. Based on this verse, how would you describe God's love?

Look up the following verses. Next to each reference, write a word that best describes God's love based on that Scripture.

Psalm 13:5

Isaiah 43:4

Isaiah 62:4–5

Lamentations 3:22–23

REFLECT

Go back through the list of verses above and read over the words you wrote next to each reference. How do those qualities of God's love make you feel?

I challenge you to do some introspective work. What are some reasons you might have a hard time feeling loved by God?

Read John 17:23, 26. We believe that God the Father loves and adores Jesus, His Son. According to Christ's prayer, how does God feel about you compared to how He feels about His own Son?

MEMORIZE

Review Ephesians 3:17b–19. Write those verses here.

PRAISE

As we close today, I want to end with a few tangible tips for praising God for His love (choose one, a few, or all):

- Keep a list of your favorite Bible verses that describe God's love. When you feel lonely, take a moment and read through them and thank God for the truth of each one.
- Listen to worship music that celebrates God's love. As you listen, praise God for His love.
- Keep a blessings list. Add one or two blessings daily that speak of Christ's love to you.
- Make a collage using photos and images that remind you of God's lavish love for you.

End your praise time today by listening to "One Thing Remains" by Kristian Stanfill.

COME HUNGRY
THERE'S MORE THAN ENOUGH

I remember the conversation like it was yesterday. My husband Steve and I had only been married for a few months, and we sat across the table from one another having a heated discussion. My Prince Charming, who wasn't being very charming, stroked his chin, looked thoughtful, and then said words no young bride wants to hear: "Becky, I think you're a little high maintenance in the love department!"

Ouch!

I don't remember how I responded; I only remember how I felt. Devastated.

Silently I prayed, "God, what's wrong with me? Why do I want to be loved so badly? Why do I want to feel like Steve is constantly pursuing me?"

Looking back, there were a lot of reasons, not the least of which was the sexual abuse I experienced as a child. Author and Bible teacher Beth Moore writes, "Childhood traumas do a terrible disservice to the memory. They scribble helter-skelter over moments of simplicity, innocence, warmth, and beauty."[7]

Certainly that was the case in my life. The abuse left holes in my heart that I couldn't begin to describe to anyone. It left me feeling needy.

Ugh. Needy wasn't something I wanted to be! Who wants to be known as needy? The truth is, though, Steve was needy too. We both came to our marriage with a trunk full of emotional baggage.

It's ironic, isn't it? Neediness in others irks us, but sometimes we're blind to our own neediness. We're all needy. As C. S. Lewis wrote, "Our whole being, by its very nature, is one vast need; incomplete, preparatory, empty yet cluttered, crying out to Him who can untie things that are now knotted together and tie up things that are still dangling loose."[8]

The great thing is that Jesus is not intimidated by our neediness. I can think of mornings when I have come into His presence and said, "Lord, I'm just a mess this morning. I overslept. I don't feel like reading my Bible. I feel frantic, frazzled, and a bit like I might cry." In those moments, Christ doesn't judge me. He simply invites me to bring my mess to His feet.

One reason Christ is not intimidated by our neediness is because His love is unlimited.

EXPLORE

Let's look again at John 6:35. "I am the bread of life. Whoever comes to me will never go hungry, and whoever believes in me will never be thirsty." Read the verse several times slowly. Circle the word "comes."

In its original Greek form, the word "comes" is in the present continuous tense.[9] In other words, Jesus is saying, if you want to experience my love, don't just limit it to one encounter; keep coming!

The supply of God's love never runs out. How cool is that? It reminds me of when my kids were infants. I would lift them to my breast, and they would frantically root around until they latched on. After they had nursed their fill, they were peaceful and content—but only for a few hours. Their tears let me know it was time to feed them again. I never resented their coming to me for more milk, though sometimes I worried that my milk supply would run out.

The other day, my little five-year-old grandson asked his mama to give him some of her "heart milk" so he could store some up for his baby brother. My daughter felt confused until she realized that he was talking about her breast milk. What a beautiful illustration of God's love for you. "Heart milk" that never runs dry. You can come and be nourished continuously.

Look up the following verses. What do each of them have to say about the supply of God's love?

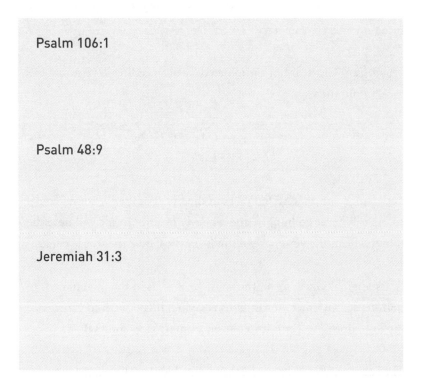

Psalm 106:1

Psalm 48:9

Jeremiah 31:3

REFLECT

Not only will Christ's love supply never run out, but also nothing can separate us from His supply. We can't out-want Him. We can't out-love Him. We can't out-pursue Him. He continuously wants us more. He continuously loves us more. And He continuously pursues us more than we can even imagine.

Think about that.

Have you ever wanted a relationship with someone more than he or she wanted it with you? How did that make you feel?

Jesus wants you to be fully assured that He wants you more than you want Him! Staggering to think about, huh? Yet, as humans our emotions go up and down, not to mention our hormones. Sometimes we'll go through seasons where we simply don't feel God's love as much as we'd like. During the seasons when you find it difficult to feel God's love, cling to the truth taught in Romans 8:38–39.

Write out those verses in the space below.

What do those verses mean to you personally?

PRAISE

Today, take a few extra minutes. Turn on some worship music from any artist or group you love.

Grab some colored pencils or markers, and write Ephesians 3:17b–21 in all different colors. Create a picture out of the verse that will remind you of how deeply you're loved by God.

Throughout your day, pause every hour and verbally affirm, "Lord Jesus, my Bread of Life, thank you for loving me completely. I praise You that I can come to You as often as I choose, as needy as I am, for more of your love."

THE MYSTERY OF BEING SATISFIED

At the beginning of this week, we looked at Jesus' question to the disciples, "Do you still not understand?" Of this we can be certain, Jesus wants you to understand and internalize His great love for you. Hasn't it been fun to dig down deep and explore His love for you?

As we end this week, today is going to be more focused on personal reflection, because I want to be sure that before we leave this *I Am* statement, you have grown in your ability to internalize God's deep love for you. I want to be sure you've moved the truth of His love for you from your head down deep into your heart—the place where you *feel* loved!

EXPLORE

Read John 6:35.

I would suggest that you read it several times, slowly and carefully. "I am the bread of life. Whoever comes to me will never go hungry, and whoever believes in me will never be thirsty." Let's review a bit of what we've unpacked in that statement.

God doesn't love you just because He has to. No, He's madly in love with you. He shows us this in a thousand different ways throughout Scripture.

Review each of the truths below, and read each correlating verse.

He sings and rejoices over you (Zeph. 3:17).
He calls you precious and honored (Isa. 43:4).
He designed you in your mother's womb (Ps. 139:13).
He comforts us like a mama when we're sad (Isa. 66:13).
He loves us with everlasting love and continuously pursues us
(Jer. 31:3).

Out of those verses, which resonates with your heart most deeply
about Christ's love?

Read Ephesians 3:14–21.

This week we've focused on memorizing Ephesians 3:17b–19, which
is tucked away in the middle of that passage. In his prayer for the
Ephesian believers, Paul prays the Holy Spirit would strengthen them
in the inner being so their faith would be more established and so
they would know how deep God's love is for them. The idea behind
the Greek word for "know" that is used here is the idea of experiencing and knowing something as fully as you can possibly know it.

REFLECT

How might the Holy Spirit help you push the enormity of God's love for you into your heart more deeply? Is there anything you can do to cooperate with Him in the process?

Moses wrote in Psalm 90:14: "Satisfy us in the morning with your unfailing love, that we may sing for joy and be glad all our days."

Think about your life at this moment. Do you feel satisfied with Christ's love? Why or why not?

After studying Jesus as the Bread of Life, what do you think it looks like to be satisfied with Christ's love when your health is failing, your finances are suffering, or you're walking through grief?

The mystery of feeling satisfied with God's love is that the more you feel satisfied, the more you want.

- When you come to Jesus as the Bread of Life, don't just nibble.
- Come to Him daily, and feast on His love.
- Consume His love messages from the Word.
- Celebrate His love through your praise.
- Focus on His love every morning when you wake up, and meditate on His love every evening as you fall asleep.

As you move through your day, whenever you feel an ache in your soul for more love, praise and thank Him that He loves you more than you could imagine. As you train your mind to focus on His love, I believe your emotions will follow, and you will feel His love more deeply.

As we close out this week, declare the words found in Psalm 63:5 over your life, "I will be fully satisfied as with the richest of foods; with singing lips my mouth will praise you."

GOD'S LOVE LETTER TO YOU

> *My precious child, I have called you by name. You are precious to me (Isa. 43:4). Before you were born, I knew you and designed you for relationship with Me (Ps. 139:13). I have loved you with a love that is eternal (Jer. 31:3) and unfailing (Ps. 107:8). Nothing you do can separate you from my love (Rom. 8:37–39). Ask me boldly for a deeper experience of my love. I delight to answer your prayer!*

MEMORIZE

Review Ephesians 3:17b–19. Write the words out on an index card, and keep the card in a place where you will see it often. Throughout your day review the words, and pray that the Holy Spirit will push the words deeper into your heart.

PRAISE

Choose your favorite song from this past week and listen to it. As you listen, soak in God's unfailing love for you!

why are you so afraid?

He replied, "You of little faith, why are you so afraid?"
Then he got up and rebuked the winds and the waves,
and it was completely calm.

MATTHEW 8:26

He said to his disciples, "Why are you so afraid?
Do you still have no faith?"

MARK 4:40

I AM THE GOOD SHEPHERD

"I am the good shepherd. The good shepherd lays down
his life for the sheep."

JOHN 10:11

WEEK 3 | DAY 1

WHY ARE YOU SO AFRAID?

MATTHEW 8:26, MARK 4:40

> *We want Christ to hurry and calm the storm.*
> *He wants us to find him in the midst of it first.*
> Beth Moore

While riding a boat across the Sea of Galilee, I looked out over the rippling water to capture the beautiful scene in my mind. As we glided along, the wind began to pick up, and the water became rough and choppy. The boat began to rock and dip. I closed my eyes and tried to imagine what it felt like for the disciples. Our guide explained the winds often came from both the east and west over the sea and that such winds could create a squall to produce waves of upwards of ten feet. I stood and leaned against the railing as my mind traveled back to the disciples and one of my favorite stories.

After a long day of ministry as the sun was just beginning to set, the disciples and Jesus climbed in a boat to cross the lake. Jesus had been teaching all day. The crowd that had gathered to hear Him was once again enormous. Many in the surrounding areas of the Sea of Galilee were pagan and found Jesus' teaching intriguing. He had taught four different stories: the parable of the sower, the parable of the lamp on a stand, the parable of the growing seed, and the parable of the mustard seed. Phew!

I know how tired I am after a long day of teaching. It's fun but exhausting. Leaving the crowd behind, Jesus and His friends set off for the other side of the Sea of Galilee. Jesus made Himself comfortable, curled up in the boat, and took a nap. Don't you love that Jesus, being fully God but also fully human, got tired? I sure do! Let's explore what happened next.

EXPLORE

Read Mark 4:35–41 several times. Write your observations and reflections in the space below.

Read Mark 4:37. Circle the phrase "furious squall" in your Bible. Using the phrase "furious squall" as a metaphor for the storms of life, what is the furious squall in your life right now?

The waves were high and the boat was taking on water fast! The boat was in danger of being swamped. Storms in our lives can create in us the feeling of being swamped as well. Looking at storms through human eyes, it can look as though we're going to drown.

Think about a time in your life when you felt so overwhelmed that you felt as though you might go under. Describe that time in the space below.

Though the storm was kicking up huge waves, Jesus lay peacefully sleeping with His head resting on a pillow.

Read Mark 4:38. Describe how the disciples felt about the fact that Jesus was sleeping.

When difficult circumstances create chaotic storms in our lives, we are tempted to feel abandoned by God. The first question we bring to the Almighty is, "Don't you care?"

Why do you think our minds are so quick to jump to the conclusion that God doesn't care?

Read Mark 4:39–40.

Jesus got up and "rebuked" the wind and spoke directly to the waves, telling them to "Be still!" Instantly, the wind and the waves obeyed His voice. Then Jesus turned to His beloved disciples and gently asked,

Why are you so afraid?

Underline that question in your Bible. Then put yourself in the disciples' position: why do you think they felt so afraid?

Then Jesus asked a follow-up question. Read Mark 4:40. Write out the question here.

Read Mark 4:41. Circle the word "terrified" in your Bible. Why do you think the disciples were terrified *after* they saw Jesus quiet the wind and the waves?

Jesus invited the disciples to look at the way the wind and the waves had just obeyed His voice and evaluate their faith. I believe that God knows we are going to feel fear in certain situations. But I also believe that He calls us to trust His care for us in our fear. In order to trust that He's not going to let us drown, we must focus on His power and love.

One way to strengthen your faith is to look back at His faithfulness in the past. This provides renewed trust for today.

In the space below look back over the last five years and think about some of the significant ways God has provided for you and demonstrated His care. Write a few of those in the space below. Date each one with the year it happened. Then write out a statement next to each explaining how this shows He cares for you. For example: God provided money for a down payment for a house in an unexpected way—2015. I realized I didn't have to feel fearful of where we'd live, because God took care of our need.

REFLECT

What situations in your life stir up fear in you?

The disciples had the privilege of watching Jesus speak directly to the wind and waves. They witnessed with shock as creation obeyed its Creator.

In what ways have you witnessed the power of God in your life?

How does a deeper understanding of Christ's power lead us toward deeper trust in Christ's protection?

Remember the kit of emergency verses you created for times of crisis in Week 1? Add a few more verses specifically for times when you feel fearful.

Read the following verses. Then choose three of the verses to include in your emergency kit. Write a sentence next to those three stating why you chose that one. Then choose one to memorize.

Joshua 1:9

Isaiah 43:1

Psalm 23:4

Psalm 43:4

Psalm 27:1

Romans 8:38–39

MEMORIZE

Begin to memorize Psalm 23:1–4. Write out the words in the space below.

PRAISE

Listen to "It Is Well" (Live) by Bethel Music and Kristene DiMarco. As you listen, spend time praising God that the wind and waves still obey His voice.

WEEK 3 | DAY 2

WHEN YOU FEEL AFRAID, YOU NEED A GOOD SHEPHERD

I remember being diagnosed with breast cancer. Fear doesn't begin to describe the vast wave of emotions I felt. Beyond fear I worried about whether or not I would be alive to finish raising my children, how my body would look after a double mastectomy, and how I would manage my schedule with so many doctor appointments. How would cancer change my life?

Soon after I was diagnosed, I was speaking at a women's conference and stayed in the home of a woman who had an intriguing painting on the wall. The painting depicted a shepherd snuggling a little lamb close to his heart. The lamb's head was nestled down deep against the Shepherd's breast where I felt quite sure the sheep could hear the rhythm of the Shepherd's heartbeat. I studied the picture for a long time. That lamb looked so safe and secure in the Shepherd's arms. She had nothing to worry about and nothing to fear.

Silently, I whispered, "Lord Jesus, you are my Good Shepherd. I feel so afraid. I want to feel safely snuggled in your arms. I want to feel protected. Please, Good Shepherd, quiet my fear and reassure me that you're holding me close."

Why are you so afraid?
I Am the Good Shepherd

Years later (and by the way, I am now seventeen years cancer free), a friend gave me an angel figurine of a shepherd holding a little lamb. That figurine sits on the dresser of my bedroom, and every time I see it, I am reminded of how my Good Shepherd quieted my fears and held me close during my cancer journey.

Life is full of fearful events, and that is exactly why we need to know our Good Shepherd. When He whispers ever so gently, "Why are you so afraid?" we can snuggle in close, pour out our hearts, and ask Him to reassure us of His presence and goodness. There in His presence, we begin to understand that He is not like any other shepherd; He alone is completely good! Let's explore the implications of His claim to be the Good Shepherd.

EXPLORE

Read John 10:1–18. Write down your observations.

A little background goes a long way toward helping us to understand this passage. In this chapter, Jesus was using a shepherd as a metaphor for leadership. In Middle Eastern culture, paralleling leaders with shepherds was easily understood. Shepherding was a common occupation. Throughout the Old Testament, Jewish leaders were often referred to as shepherds, so at the time of Jesus, people would have been familiar with this concept. Even those who were pagan would be able to understand that shepherds took loving care of their sheep because their sheep were valuable.

Throughout John 10, the word that's used for shepherd is *poimĕn* in the Greek. It means a herdsman shepherd who tends, leads, guides, cherishes, feeds, and protects the flock (Strong's #4166).

To gain a better understanding of this passage, let's take a look at Ezekiel 34 where the prophet chastised the false shepherds of Israel and prophesied the coming of the Messiah as the true Shepherd.

Read Ezekiel 34:1–6. List the accusations that the Lord brings against the shepherds of Israel.

Read Ezekiel 34:11–16. What promises does God make about shepherding His own people?

Read Ezekiel 34:31. Write out this verse in your own words.

Read John 10:11. What is the distinctive mark of the Good Shepherd?

How is the Good Shepherd different from the shepherds of Israel?

In this powerful *I Am* statement, Jesus shows His full provision for His sheep. As we continue through this week, you're going to discover that the Good Shepherd leads, protects, guides, feeds, and lays down His life for His sheep.

REFLECT

In thinking about leaders you've known, how many leaders lead through intimidation? Have you ever been hurt by this type of leadership? If so, write about it.

How is Jesus' style of leadership different and unique?

What does it mean to you, personally, that the Good Shepherd laid down His life for you?

MEMORIZE

Review Psalm 23:1–4.

PRAISE

Listen to "Shepherd" (Live) by Bethel Music and Amanda Cook. As you listen, worship and praise Jesus Christ that He is your Good Shepherd.

A PORTRAIT OF THE GOOD SHEPHERD

What you have in your shepherd
is greater than what you don't have in life.
—Max Lucado

Many years ago, my ten-year-old daughter's journal lay open on her bedroom floor as Steve and I knelt beside her bed, ready to tuck her in and pray with her. I asked Keri if I could read what she had written. The first few lines tore my heart wide open:

Dear God,
I always thought nothing bad could ever happen to my family.
Now my mom has breast cancer. How could You let this happen?
I'm afraid, God!

The anguish and fear behind Keri's words brought fresh tears to my eyes. Hours before we had shared the news with our four kids, the doctor had called to tell us that the biopsy revealed aggressive cancer in several areas and that I would need a double mastectomy. Fear enveloped me as I shared the news. I wanted to be the calm and strong mom who could reassure her kids everything was going to be fine. But I wasn't sure.

I felt a strange sense of foreboding. Doubt and fear assaulted my mind. Silently, I prayed, "Oh, Father, help us! Our kids are so frightened. I don't want them to walk away from you as we journey through this dark valley. Please give Steve and me wisdom. Show me what it looks like to nestle into you, the Good Shepherd." It was the perfect time to return to an old, comforting favorite, Psalm 23.

EXPLORE

Read Psalm 23. Write your observations in the space below.

David, the author of Psalm 23, understood the meaning of fear. He lived for many years under the shadow of Saul's threats to take his life. Though at one point Saul viewed David as a surrogate son, his affection turned to jealousy after David killed Goliath and the crowds began praising David, saying, "Saul has slain his thousands, and David his tens of thousands!" (1 Sam. 18:7).

Countless times David narrowly escaped Saul's anger and death threats. No wonder so many of David's psalms address fear.

David also knew a lot about sheep and shepherding. As a teenager he had shepherded his father's sheep. In Psalm 23, he beautifully painted the portrait of the Lord as his shepherd.

Read Psalm 23:1. Underline the phrase, "The Lord."

David's wording is significant. *Yahweh*, the Hebrew word for "Lord," is the most personal, intimate name God assigned to Himself.[10] *Rohpi* is the Hebrew word for shepherd and describes God as the one who provides loving care.[11]

Circle the word "my." What does it mean to you that the Lord, the God of the universe, the One who wants a deep friendship with you and the One who provides loving care, is your personal shepherd? Write out your thoughts below. How would your life look different if you really believed that?

In Psalm 23, David writes prophetically giving us five promises we can count on from our Good Shepherd to help quiet fear.

1. The Good Shepherd promises to provide for your needs.

Read Psalm 23:1. Look up the following verses, and write the promise of each one in your own words.

Psalm 34:10

Psalm 84:11

Luke 12:24

Philippians 4:13

2. The Good Shepherd promises to restore your soul.

Read Psalm 23:2–3. While the shepherd promises to provide soul restoration, it doesn't happen without rest. Why do you think our culture rebels against rest?

Read Psalm 46:10. What does this verse say to you about rest?

Read Exodus 20:8–11. Why do you think God gave us the principle of Sabbath rest?

Sabbath is a foreign language to the native tongue
Of a busy culture,
A curious oddity in an overtired church.
—Shelly Miller

Think about your life. How great is your need for rest at this present time? What are you doing about that need?

3. The Good Shepherd promises to guide you.

Read Psalm 23:3. Underline in your Bible the part of the verse that specifically promises the Shepherd's guidance.

Change can trigger fear in some. But guess what? Sheep don't like change either! Who knew? Sheep are creatures of habit. If they stay in the same spot grazing for too long, the area becomes infested with parasites. So, shepherds keep their sheep moving! In biblical times, the shepherd went ahead of the sheep preparing the grasslands where the sheep would graze. He picked all the weeds and uprooted anything that could potentially poison the sheep.

The same holds true in our lives. Our Shepherd knows how beneficial change is for our spiritual growth. Therefore, He is faithfully leading us on to new pastures of challenge. But He goes before us preparing the way.

As I write this, Steve and I have just journeyed through a season of change. Several months ago, we left the pastorate after 35 years, and Steve stepped in as the CEO of Reach Beyond, a ministry seeking to empower partners together to be the voice and hands of Jesus globally. In the months leading up to the change, I noticed some anxiety in my soul.

Many days I prayed, "Lord, thank you that you go before, behind, above, and beneath us into this new season." Looking back, the Shepherd knew what He was doing. (No kidding, right?) Steve is happier than ever in his new role, and God has opened doors for me that I never dreamed possible.

Read Psalm 37:23. What does it look like for you to delight in the Lord during seasons of transition?

4. The Good Shepherd promises to be with you in the dark valley.

Read Psalm 23:4. Because we live in a fallen world, each of us will face dark valleys. Have you been through a dark valley recently? Describe that below. How might the Shepherd's presence quiet fear in those valleys?

5. The Good Shepherd promises to comfort you when you face evil.

Read Psalm 23:4. The Shepherd doesn't promise to always protect us from evil, but what He does promise is that He will be with us when we face evil. How is this promise comforting to you?

REFLECT

Which of the five promises most resonates with you? Why?

Is change challenging or exciting for you? How does knowing the Shepherd goes before you into every new situation comfort and reassure your heart?

MEMORIZE

Review Psalm 23:1–4.

PRAISE

Write out your own version of Psalm 23, and then use your psalm as a pattern for your praise. For example, your psalm might begin something like this:

"The Lord is my Shepherd, I don't have to be afraid.
He provides for all my needs: physical, emotional, and spiritual."

HE KNOWS YOUR NAME.
DO YOU KNOW HIS VOICE?

As I write this, Steve and I are visiting our Reach Beyond office in England. As we've driven through the English countryside, we've seen sheep grazing on the hillside. I've wondered, "Where is their shepherd?" And, "How does their shepherd get them all back home at night?" They seem to wander aimlessly around the grassy landscape of England.

Intrigued, I asked our friends. I found out that the shepherds use sheepherding dogs and all-terrain vehicles to corral the sheep. Who knew? That makes shepherding sound so fun! Sometimes the sheep-herding dogs actually jump on the back of the ATVs and ride along with the shepherd.

In central Asia, the sheep know the shepherd's voice, and they re-spond accordingly. That's a bit more in line with the Middle Eastern culture in which Jesus taught. Jesus said, as the Good Shepherd, He calls His sheep by name and that His sheep know His voice.

EXPLORE

Read John 10:3b–4. Write these two verses out in the space below. Underline the phrase "He calls his own sheep by name." In what way does this affirm to you that Jesus desires a personal intimate relationship with you?

Read Isaiah 43:1 (ESV). Write out the phrases "I have called you by name, you are mine" in the space below. How does this verse speak to you?

Read John 10:4. Circle the phrase "they know his voice." On a scale of 1 (least likely to recognize) to 10 (most likely to recognize), how good are you at discerning the voice of God?

Read 1 Samuel 3:1–9. What lesson can you learn from this story?

Read John 20:11–18. Why do you think Mary didn't recognize Jesus' voice until He spoke her name?

Scripture teaches us that we can recognize God's voice in several ways.

Look up each of the following verses. Next to each verse write down what the passage teaches you about discerning God's voice:

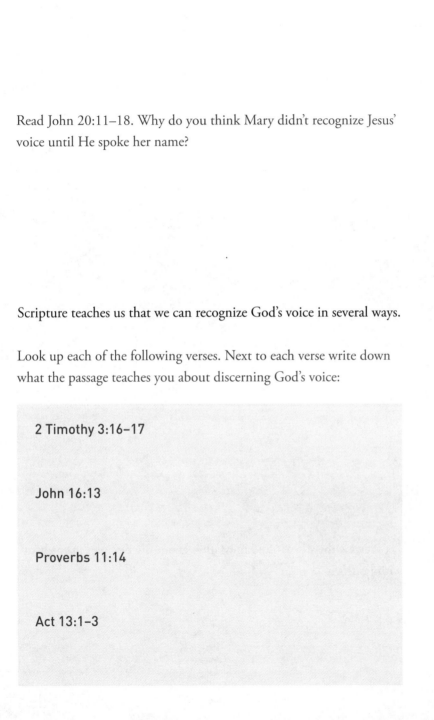

2 Timothy 3:16–17

John 16:13

Proverbs 11:14

Act 13:1–3

REFLECT

Do you believe the Good Shepherd knows you by name and wants to communicate with you? Why or why not?

As you reflect back on the Scriptures you've studied today, what is one truth that stands out to you?

How might God's voice quiet fear in your heart?

Let's review the story found in Mark 4 about the disciples in the boat with Jesus.

Read Mark 4:39–40. Notice the wind and the waves recognized the voice of God immediately, and instantly they obeyed. In thinking about recognizing the voice of the Good Shepherd, what is the lesson for us?

How can you cultivate a willingness to listen and obey God's voice? Write a prayer of commitment below.

MEMORIZE

Review Psalm 23:1–4.

PRAISE

Listen to "Speak to Me" by Kari Jobe. As you listen, make this your prayer.

ABUNDANT LIFE = COURAGEOUS LIFE

We've come a long way this week, haven't we?

- We began with the question that Jesus asked, "Why are you so afraid?"
- We explored His claim that He is the Good Shepherd.
- We've looked at the portrait that David painted for us of the Good Shepherd and the promises that come with that to quiet our fears.
- We've discovered that Jesus calls us by name and longs for us to know His voice.
- And we've looked at how recognizing His voice can help quiet our fears.

Today, we're going to look at the abundant life that Jesus promised. In a world filled with violence, terrorist attacks, sickness, and poverty, what did Jesus mean by abundant life?

EXPLORE

Read John 10:10. Think through the different definitions or explanations of an abundant life that you've heard. Write some of those ideas below.

Jesus said, "I have come that they may have life, and have it to the full." The Greek word for life used here is zōḗ—"life," physical and spiritual (Strong's #2222). What's interesting about this word is that it means life originated and sustained from God. It implies that the Lord *intimately shares* His gift of life with *people* and gives them the capacity to know and experience His eternal life.

In some versions of the Bible, the phrase "have it to the full" has been translated "abundant." In the Greek the word is *perissós*, and it carries the idea of "superabundance, excessive, overflowing, surplus, over and above, more than enough, profuse, extraordinary, above the ordinary, more than sufficient" (Strong's #4053). Many feel the word is speaking of financial blessing. That's possible, but I think Jesus had way more in mind. What if an abundant life was a life lived boldly and confidently with passion and purpose for the honor of Jesus Christ? Isn't that what you want?

Fear can hold us captive and prevent us from living the abundant life Christ offers. But I believe that while fear may never completely vanish, an abundant, bold life is possible.

Imagine being so confident in Christ's love that you no longer wrestle with insecurity. Imagine being so sure of Christ's presence that you experience deep-seated peace even in the dark valley. Imagine being so bold for the cause of Christ that you tell others about Him readily and without fear.

Read 1 John 4:18. How might fear rob us of the abundant life Christ offers?

How might a deeper understanding of Christ's love quiet fear in your life?

Read Romans 8:35–39. In these verses, the apostle Paul writes about bold confidence in God's love. How do these verses give you a deeper understanding of the abundant life Christ promised?

REFLECT

As you think back on this week and all that we've studied about the Good Shepherd, how might your life look differently, if you truly believed He was good and His every intention toward you was good? How might fear fade and courage emerge?

Think about a person you admire who lives an abundant life. What specific qualities do you admire about that person? Do you think those qualities are possible for you? Why or why not?

What truth about the Shepherd's care most impacted you this week? Why?

How do you listen for the Shepherd's voice?

Consider for a moment, what is your worst fear? How does knowing the Good Shepherd calm that fear?

MEMORIZE

Review Psalm 23:1–4.

PRAISE

Write a prayer of praise thanking Jesus for offering abundant life. Then listen to "Not Afraid" by Mosaic. As you listen, praise God that an abundant, bold life is possible for you because of Jesus.

what do you want me to do for you?

"What do you want me to do for you?" Jesus asked him.
The blind man said, "Rabbi, I want to see."

MARK 10:51

I AM THE LIGHT

When Jesus spoke again to the people, he said, "I am the light of the world. Whoever follows me will never walk in darkness, but will have the light of life."

JOHN 8:12

WEEK 4 | DAY 1

WHAT DO YOU WANT ME TO DO FOR YOU?

MARK 10:51

The only thing worse than being blind
is having sight but no vision.
—Helen Keller

Janet is one of my most remarkable friends. She lost her eyesight at age 30 as she was trying to raise three little boys. Her husband, unable to cope with all the stress, walked out on their marriage. Can you imagine?

In desperate search of healing, Janet decided to attend a church service. She did in fact receive healing, but not the kind she was hoping for! Instead, she heard about Jesus, how much He loved her, and how He wanted relationship with her—how He would never leave her. That day Janet put her faith and trust in Jesus Christ. Everything began to change! Her eyesight wasn't restored, but Janet became filled with courage and boldness to navigate life blind, but fulfilled! Soon after her conversion, her husband, Gene, returned to her and their family and eventually found the Lord.

Janet and Gene are dear friends and have an amazing testimony for the Lord. Though blind, Janet sees Jesus with incredible clarity. She travels and speaks to audiences all over the world about Jesus and how He can empower people to overcome life's greatest challenges.

Being blind today is a challenge, but being blind at the time of Jesus' earthly life was even more difficult. People at the time of Christ looked down on those who were blind. They viewed them as not only disabled but also incompetent. In fact, many believed that if you were blind, it was because God was punishing you for a sin you had committed. The blind had little opportunity to earn a living and often became beggars. That was the situation for Bartimaeus.

EXPLORE

Read Mark 10:46–52. Read the passage several times, and write down your observations in the space below.

Read Mark 10:48. Describe Bartimaeus's attitude in your own words.

How would you describe the attitude of the crowd?

How do people today mistreat those with disabilities?

Read Mark 10:48. What was Bartimaeus's response to being scolded?

Read Mark 10:49. In your Bible, circle the phrase "Jesus stopped." What does Jesus' action tell you about His heart to listen to broken people?

Jesus called Bartimaeus, and immediately Bartimaeus jumped to his feet, threw his coat off, and came to Jesus.

How would you describe Bartimaeus's attitude here?

With Bartimaeus before Him, Jesus asked one of my favorite questions ever! "What do you want me to do for you?" Can you imagine? The King of Kings and the Lord of Lords looking at you and asking:

What do you want me to do for you?

How would you answer His question?

Bartimaeus answered, "I want to see." Jesus answered, "Go, your faith has healed you." Faith means "conviction, confidence, trust, and belief" (Strong's #4102).

What evidence do you see of Bartimaeus's faith?

Describe some of the changes that Bartimaeus likely experienced as a result of this miracle.

REFLECT

Think about Bartimaeus's answer "I want to see." Adapt that answer to fit your own life circumstances. How would you complete this sentence in the space below? I want to see . . . (You might say, I want to see how deeply you love me. Or I want to see your purpose for my life. Or I want to see your movement in my marriage.)

Read Mark 11:24. Life can feel dark at times. What assurance do you have that, just as Jesus heard Bartimaeus's cry for mercy, He also hears the cries of your heart?

MEMORIZE

Memorize John 1:1–5. Write the verses in the space below.

PRAISE

Listen to "Listen to Our Hearts" by Casting Crowns. As you listen, praise God that He knows every longing of your heart.

WEEK 4 | DAY 2

WHEN LIFE FEELS DARK, YOU NEED THE LIGHT

I was sitting at a Starbucks in California, and a young woman was seated at a nearby table. All of a sudden she threw down the newspaper she was reading and yelled, "Gosh! The world is a dark place! What the heck is going on?" With that, she stormed away from Starbucks.

She's definitely right! The newspaper that day was filled with stories of terrorist attacks—one in London and one in Mali—fights between political parties, murders, and a few other dark stories. It's true. The world is a very dark place. In stark contrast to the darkness surrounding us stands Jesus, who claimed to be the Light of the World. I don't know about you, but that makes my heart sing!

Jesus actually claimed to be the Light of the World twice, just to be sure we understood. Today, we'll look at His first claim, and tomorrow, we'll look at His second claim.

What do you want me to do for you?
I Am the Light of the World

EXPLORE

Read John 8:12–20.

Jesus was in Jerusalem for the Feast of Tabernacles when He made this statement (John 7:14). To understand what a significant festival this was, let's look at some background.

Every year in late summer or early fall, the Israelites traveled to Jerusalem for the Feast of Tabernacles. They spent seven days feasting and celebrating. Sounds like fun, huh? God had given them the holiday so that the Jews would never forget what He had done for them during their forty years wandering in the wilderness. During their time in the wilderness, God led them by a cloud during the day and by a pillar of fire at night so that they would always be able to see where they were going.

Read Exodus 13:21–22. What did the pillar of the cloud and the pillar of the fire each represent?

Write out Exodus 13:21–22 in the space below.

On the last day of the Feast of Tabernacles, the Day of the Great Hosanna, a specially-appointed priest poured water from a golden pitcher over a rock, symbolizing God's provision of water that gushed from the rock in the wilderness. When the priests poured out the water, there was a loud blast of trumpets, and the choirs and crowds of people formed processions singing praises to God.

Jesus chose this exact moment—when passion was filling the temple and the crowds were singing praises to God—to make His bold declaration, "I am the light of the world" (John 8:12).

I'm pretty sure His words stopped the crowd. They knew exactly what Jesus was saying. He was the light that had led them through the wilderness. God Himself!

Read John 8:12. What did Jesus promise with His claim of being the Light of the World?

Read John 8:14–19. What is Jesus claiming about Himself in these verses? What is the implication of Jesus saying, "I stand with the Father, who sent me"?

Read John 8:23, 24, 48–59.

After Jesus proclaimed that He was the Light of the World, He made some other bold statements about His identity and eternality. Several of these statements correlate with prophecies Isaiah made years before about the coming Messiah.

Look up each prophecy below, and write a statement about what the prophecy says about Jesus.

Isaiah 41:4

Isaiah 43:10

Isaiah 46:4

Read John 8:58–59. Describe the response of the religious leaders.

Why do you think the Pharisees were so upset with Jesus?

Throughout Scripture, good and evil and chaos and clarity are contrasted by light and darkness. "Darkness" in both the Old Testament (Heb. *hasak*) and New Testament (*skotos*) is an evocative word. If light symbolizes God, darkness connotes everything that is anti-God: the wicked (Prov. 2:13–14; 1 Thess. 5:4–7), judgment (Ex. 10:21; Matt. 25:30), and death (Ps. 88:12). Salvation brings light to those in darkness (Isa. 9:2).[12] Jesus came as the exact opposite of everything that is dark! His very nature screams light and salvation.

Look up each verse. Then write one or two words to describe darkness and one or two words to describe how God brings light.

SCRIPTURE	LIGHT	DARKNESS
Genesis 1:1–2		
Psalm 18:28		
Isaiah 9:1–2		
John 1:4–5, 9		
Ephesians 5:8–11		

REFLECT

What does it mean to you that Jesus came as the Light of the World?

What did you learn today about God's presence?

Where do you most need God's guidance at this point in your life?

Read Psalm 32:8. Write out this promise in your own words.

Write out a prayer expressing your need for Christ's light in your life.

MEMORIZE

Write out John 1:1–4 below, then test yourself on how well you're remembering it.

PRAISE

Listen to "Light of the World" by Lauren Daigle. As you listen, praise Jesus that as the Light of the World, He will guide and direct you as He's promised.

FROM OUTCAST TO CELEBRITY

Sometimes God allows what he hates to accomplish what he loves.
—Joni Eareckson Tada

After Jesus left the temple where He was celebrating the Feast of Tabernacles, He walked along with His disciples. Imagine the conversation they had reflecting on how upset the religious leaders had been with Jesus. The leaders had almost stoned Jesus to death. Had it not been for God Himself hiding Jesus, they would have succeeded.

As Jesus and His disciples walked along, they came across another blind beggar. Immediately, the disciples jumped to some very rough conclusions about this disabled man. Isn't it amazing how quickly we jump to conclusions and judge situations and people based on our human wisdom rather than by God's wisdom? Jesus' disciples assumed that either the blind man or his parents had sinned and that's why the beggar had lost his sight. How insensitive. Praise God, Jesus always had a heart for the disabled, the poor, the broken, the messy, and the marginalized! Let's take a look.

EXPLORE

Read John 9:1–5.

The disciples asked Jesus why the man was born blind and erroneously concluded that either he had sinned or his parents had sinned.

Describe how Jesus answered them.

How does the attitude of the disciples compare with those in the crowd who told Bartimaeus to "Be quiet!"

Why do you think God allows people to suffer?

Read verse 4 once again. What do you think Jesus meant by "day," and what do you think He meant by using the word "night"?

Read verse 5 again, and underline the *I Am* statement Jesus made.

Read John 9:6–7.

Describe how Jesus healed the man. Why do you think Jesus used His saliva to heal the man's eyes?

The pool of Siloam had been built by King Hezekiah to provide for those in Jerusalem in case of a siege against the city. If the city were ever under attack, those living in Jerusalem would have water. In many ways, these waters symbolized the work that Jesus would come to do. Remember, Jesus came as the Living Water (John 4:10) to bring hope and deliverance.

When Jesus asked the man to go and wash in the pool of Siloam, it was very symbolic of the complete cleansing He wanted to accomplish in the blind man's life. Jesus came not only to open our eyes and give us sight into who He is, but also to cleanse us and make us whole.

Read John 9:11–30. Describe the reaction of the man's neighbors to the miracle Jesus had done.

Describe the reaction of the Pharisees to the miracle Jesus had done.

Read John 9:35–41.

Describe the blind man's response after he was thrown out of the synagogue.

How does this man demonstrate a genuine conversion experience?

What do you think Jesus meant when He said, "For judgment I have come into this world, so that the blind will see and those who see will become blind" (John 9:39)?

To be spiritually blind means that a person is blind to who Jesus Christ truly is—God Himself. Beyond being blind to the identity and power of Jesus Christ, a person of faith can be blind to:

- Their own shortcomings
- Where God is leading
- How God is moving
- False teaching that is not founded on the Word of God

REFLECT

How can you protect yourself from spiritual blindness?

Read Psalm 19:12. In what ways have you been guilty of being blind to your own shortcomings? Write out a prayer for God to increase your self-awareness. (Please note, we are not looking to increase our self-obsession but rather self-awareness or the ability to see our own faults.)

The blind man said, emphatically, "One thing I do know. I was blind but now I see!" (John 9:25). That statement became his testimony—his story of what God had done in his life. Your testimony—your story of what God has done in your life—can become what God uses to lead another to Himself. It's important to be able to share your story with others so that they can know Jesus too.

Write out a short version of your testimony. How has knowing Jesus opened your eyes and changed your life?

What can you learn from the boldness of the blind man in sharing his encounter with Jesus with the Pharisees?

MEMORIZE

Review John 1:1–4.

PRAISE

Listen to "Let There Be light" by Bryan and Katie Torwalt. As you listen, praise Jesus that He came as the Light of the World to illumine your darkness and bring clarity to your confusion.

WHEN YOU NEED DIRECTION, SEEK THE LIGHT

If you have light
just for the moment in which you find yourself,
It is enough…
For you have Him and He is all you need.
—Stormie Omartian

My husband has a love-hate relationship with Siri! When he asks Siri for directions, sometimes she gets it right. Other times, she gets it terribly wrong. I've seen Siri bring out the dark side of Steve. While normally a sweet, nice guy, on occasion Steve has called Siri a "bone head."

I'm not one to judge. I've become pretty frustrated with Siri myself. One time I clearly remember driving around in circles for about a half hour before I discovered that her directions had sent me on a wild goose chase! I suppose even Siri needs grace. Sigh.

While most of us now have a GPS at our fingertips, we are at times unsure of God's direction in our lives, particularly during seasons of transition. We want an answer to the question, "Where is God leading?" We want to be sure we're doing the right thing when trying to discern God's will for daily decisions such as:

- Should I buy a home or simply rent one?
- Should I move my family across the country for a better job or stay put so the kids feel secure?
- Should we put the kids in public school, Christian school, or homeschool?
- Should I get married or stay single?
- Should we stay at our present church even though we're no longer satisfied or change to a new church?
- Should we adopt or foster?

EXPLORE

Read Luke 1:79.

As the Light of the World, Jesus came to light our path and give us direction. Yet sometimes, it feels that His direction is hard to find. This is because God seems to value trust over clarity. So how do we discern God's direction in our lives?

REFLECT

Steve and I have learned the benefit of taking inventory and asking ourselves these five questions to help us discern where the Light of the World is leading. These questions are meant to help you spend time in God's presence pursuing His will. My warning is this: answers might not come quickly. Too often when we don't sense an answer from God immediately, we give up. Please don't do that. Keep seeking His will. You might return to some of the questions several times to get a clear picture of where God is leading.

Read the verses under each question to help you figure out how to best take inventory.

Take Inventory to Discern Where the Light Is Leading

1. What does God seem to be saying through my regular Bible reading?

When reading God's Word to discern direction, look for patterns. Read the following verses, and write your thoughts next to each verse about how God's Word gives us direction.

Read Psalm 119:105.

Read Proverbs 6:23.

2. What does the Holy Spirit seem to be speaking to my spirit?

Read the Scriptures below, and then write down what each verse teaches about the role of the Holy Spirit in leading us.

Read John 14:15–17.

Read John 16:13–14.

Read Acts 13:2.

3. Which option requires me to have the most faith? Read Hebrews 11:6.

4. What is the best use of my resources, spiritual gifts, and talents? Read 1 Timothy 6:17.

5. **What are my mentors and wise friends saying? Read Proverbs 15:22.**

After you've answered those questions, write down where you think God might be leading. The bottom line is that you have to take a leap of faith!

MEMORIZE

Review John 1:1–4, and write it out in the space below.

PRAISE

Listen to "Let There Be Light" by Hillsong Worship (Live). As you listen, praise Jesus that as the Light of the World. He will lead you one step at a time.

WEEK 4 | DAY 5

COMPLETE CLARITY OR TRUST?

We began this week with Jesus' question, "What do you want me to do for you?" There are times in our lives when we feel like Bartimaeus. Life seems dark. In confusion you wonder, "Where is God, and where is He leading?"

If Jesus asked you, "What do you want me to do for you?" you might scream, "Please, just make things clear! I want to follow, but I need clarity!"

Brennan Manning told this story in his profound book, *Ruthless Trust*:

> When the brilliant ethicist John Kavanaugh went to work for three months at "the house of the dying" in Calcutta, he was seeking a clear answer as to how best to spend the rest of his life. On the first morning there he met Mother Teresa. She asked, "And what can I do for you?" Kavanaugh asked her to pray for him. "What do you want me to pray for?" she asked. He voiced the request that he had borne thousands of miles from the United States: "Pray that I have clarity." She said firmly, "No, I will not do that." When he asked her why, she said, "Clarity is the last thing you are clinging to and must let go of." When Kavanaugh commented that she always seemed to have the clarity he longed for, she laughed and said, "I have never had clarity; what I have always had is trust. So I will pray that you trust God."[13]

Most of us can relate to Kavanaugh's request for clarity. We've all had moments when we've begged God to make His guidance clear. Today we're going to be looking at Jesus' claim to be the Light of the World and how His claim relates to the question, "What do you want me to do for you?"

EXPLORE

At the beginning of this week, how did you answer Jesus' question "What do you want me to do for you?" Has your answer changed at all this week?

Read John 8:12. Write the verse in the space below. Circle the second sentence of this verse. What is the promise for those who choose to follow?

Let's return to Exodus 13:21–22. What would have happened if the people had chosen to not follow the cloud or the pillar of fire?

When Jesus claimed to be the Light of the World, He clearly defined Himself as the only true light for all people. The only one who can provide clarity, revealing the Father's true nature to humanity.

Read Colossians 1:15–20. What do these verses teach you about the nature of Jesus Christ?

Not only for eternity, but also for this present life, we are promised that the light of Christ's presence will guide and direct us.

Read John 14:15 and 23. What do these verses teach about the correlation between our love for Christ and our obedience to what He commands?

Read Luke 11:28. As believers, how do we "hear" the voice of God? Do you think it's harder to hear God's voice or obey God's voice? Why?

REFLECT

What most often makes you resistant to obeying God's voice?

What part does fear play in whether or not you are willing to follow God's leading?

Are there steps you can take toward cultivating an obedient heart? If so, what are those steps?

Think back over the last week and what you've learned about Jesus as the Light of the World and His leading in your life. What is the most significant lesson you've learned?

MEMORIZE

Write out John 1:1–4 from memory in the space below.

PRAISE

Listen to "Be Thou My Vision" by Selah. As you listen, praise God that He is leading you and that even when the path is not completely clear, you can trust Him.

do you believe I am able to do this?

When he had gone indoors, the blind men came to him, and he asked them, "Do you believe that I am able to do this?" "Yes, Lord," they replied.

MATTHEW 9:28

I AM THE RESURRECTION AND THE LIFE

Jesus said to her, "I am the resurrection and the life. The one who believes in me will live, even though they die. . ."

JOHN 11:25

WEEK 5 | DAY 1

DO YOU BELIEVE THAT I AM ABLE TO DO THIS?

MATTHEW 9:28

> *The crucial issue in advancing the kingdom of God*
> *is not the quantity of our faith, but the power of God.*
> —John Piper

I love stories of great faith! They remind me that God still moves in miraculous ways.

Dr. John and Marion Slater served as missionaries with World Venture (formerly, The Conservative Baptist Mission) in the Belgian Congo from 1959–1961. Their daughter, Karen Cole, is a dear friend of mine and told me the following story:

One hot, humid day John trudged through waist-high elephant grass, hunting for wild pig or deer. Suddenly a young African boy, about 12 or 13 years old, appeared. Sweat poured down his face as he relayed the message that the chief of his village had sent him as a runner to find the white doctor who was hunting.

The chief's wife had been in labor for two days and was suffering greatly. John and the boy immediately set out to find their car and head for the village many kilometers away. After nearly an hour of dodging pot-holes in the old Land Cruiser, they finally arrived at the village. John was greeted by the chief, then was quickly taken to the hut where the wife lay. The sounds of moaning greeted him as he entered.

The air inside the hut was heavy with smoke from the wood fire in the corner, and John could barely see the woman. But as he got closer, he realized that the witch doctor had already been there because of the white markings on the woman's belly. Exhausted and weary from the contractions of labor, she gazed up at him with fear-filled eyes.

John quietly asked for a bowl of hot water and soap to wash his hands. He was praying the entire time, asking his Great Physician for wisdom. He placed his hands on the woman's belly, asking God to direct the movement of his hands so that he could figure out the problem. God was more than willing to answer, and John quickly discovered the baby was breech.

He would need to turn the baby or both mother and baby would soon die. He told the woman he was going to pray for her, a prayer to the almighty God who loved her dearly, the creator of her baby. As he soaped her belly, he could feel the Lord guide his hands as he gently turned the precious one inside the womb. He begged the Lord to keep the baby alive and give the young mother strength. After a few minutes, the contractions increased once again and in God's miraculous provision, the baby turned.

A baby boy was born, but the baby was too quiet. John held the baby close and gently massaged his limbs. Then finally, there was a cry, and a moment later, an even louder cry. Outside the hut, the chief smiled and laughed; this would be his first son. This baby would be the future chief of this village. As the tired doctor stood and thanked God, he realized he needed to say something to the village.

Incredibly, the Lord gave John the ability to speak clearly in the village's native tongue, though until that moment, he knew very little of the language. He shared the story of the gospel plainly and powerfully. People listened, shocked and amazed because they understood this man who previously had not spoken their language well. That day the chief gave his life to Christ, and many in the village also came to Christ. John chose to believe that God could do the impossible, and the power of God showed up in a mighty way!

The power of faith can be life changing and yet, when Jesus asks—

Do you believe that I am able to do this?

—many of us pause and stammer. Let's take a look at the situation where Jesus first asked this question.

EXPLORE

Read Matthew 9:27–31.

As Jesus walked along with His disciples, two blind men began crying out for mercy. It's amazing how many blind people Jesus healed during His earthly ministry, isn't it? Many years before Christ, the prophet Isaiah prophesied that when the Messiah came, "Then will the eyes of the blind be opened and the ears of the deaf unstopped" (Isa. 35:5).

How does this story validate Jesus as the Messiah?

After crying out for mercy, the blind men followed Jesus into the house. That feels like a pretty gutsy move on their part.

What do their actions show you about their determination?

Read Matthew 9:28. Write out the question Jesus asked.

There's that word again. *Believe.* In the space below write out the definition for "believe" in your own words. What is the significance of the word "believe" being a verb?

Read Hebrews 11:1. In your own words, write out what this verse teaches about faith.

Read the following verses, and write a statement next to each describing what the verse teaches about cultivating belief.

Luke 17:5

Romans 10:17

Hebrews 10:22–23

James 1:22

Read Matthew 9:29.

The blind men had proven their faith by following Jesus into the house. Jesus honored their faith and restored their sight. But it's important that we understand the words "according to your faith."

Is there any indication in Jesus' words that He healed according to the size of their faith?

Read Matthew 17:20. What does this verse teach us about the correlation between the size of our faith and the greatness of what God does?

REFLECT

In Western culture, our cynicism and skepticism can at times hinder our faith.

Since the word Jesus used for "believe" is a verb, what action steps can you take to increase your faith and decrease your cynicism?

Read Matthew 19:26. Write this verse out in the space below. Circle the word "all."

In your life, where do you need more faith to believe that with God everything is possible? Write out your thoughts.

Read Mark 9:21–24.
The boy's father cried out to Jesus, "I do believe; help me overcome my unbelief!"

Write out a prayer of your own using this man's words to express your desire for greater faith.

MEMORIZE

Begin memorizing John 11:25. Write it out in the space below.

PRAISE

Listen to "Cornerstone" by Hillsong. As you listen, praise Jesus as the solid cornerstone of your faith, the One who can do above and beyond all that you could ever dream of asking or imagining.

WHEN GOD SEEMS ALOOF

Jesus calls us to die to what's most important to us:
Our dreams, our success, our prestige, and our reputation.
In those moments He invites us to come to Him as
the resurrection and the life.
—Becky Harling

"Becky, it feels like God is aloof in my suffering. Like, He's silent and simply doesn't care."

I could hear sniffles on the other end of the phone. Rita felt beyond discouraged. She and her husband had completed their home study, and all systems were go for the adoption they had been dreaming about for years. They felt sure God was calling them. They knew His plans were good. Plane tickets had been purchased and hotels paid for as they had flown out of state to meet their precious little one. But in an unexpected turn of events, the birth mom changed her mind. To make matters worse, the baby would now be living in a community where drugs were the norm. The social worker explained that though the baby didn't stand much of a chance of being well cared for, her hands were tied. It was unthinkable. How could God not care?

Then there was Sara. She sobbed as I held her in my arms ready to pray over her. The cry escaping her lips was, "Becky, where was God? How could He let this happen?" I had no answers for my friend who had experienced horrible sexual abuse. The glib answer of "He works all things for our good" didn't feel appropriate. Instead, I held her and cried a few tears myself.

Maybe you don't have a story like Rita's or Sara's, but if truth be told, you've felt a bit disillusioned with God lately or in the past. You pray for months, and God seems silent. Now a million questions pummel your mind, "Does He care? Is He listening? Does He only do good things for other people? Is He aloof?"

I think that's the way Mary and Martha must have felt when their brother Lazarus died. Let's take a look.

> Do you believe that I am able to do this?
> *I Am* the Resurrection and the Life

EXPLORE

Read John 11:1–44.

Mary, Martha, and Lazarus were close friends of Jesus. He often stayed with them when traveling through Bethany. Mary was known for her extravagant love for Jesus. She poured perfume on the Lord and wiped His feet with her hair. (John describes this event in the next chapter, John 12:1–7). Martha was known for serving Jesus well and cooking Him great dinners. They were the kind of friends you'd spend the holidays with or go on vacation with. So when Lazarus became ill, they immediately sent word to Jesus, "Lord, the one you love is sick." The implication was clear, come quickly! This is where the story takes an unexpected twist. Jesus purposefully delays.

Read John 11:4–6.

After Jesus received the frantic message from Martha and Mary, He told his disciples that Lazarus's sickness would not end in death. The apostle John writes, "Now Jesus loved Martha and her sister and Lazarus. So when he heard Lazarus was sick he stayed where he was."

Circle the word "so." When John was writing this gospel, he had vivid memories of this event. He writes this passage in such a way that we understand that because Jesus loved Mary and Martha so much, He delayed. Makes you want to say, "What?!" Our understanding of love drives us to respond to emergencies quickly, right?

In fact, just a few weeks ago one of our daughters was in a serious car accident. Steve and I cancelled all our appointments and drove as quickly as we could to go be with her. Everyone was fine, but her car was totaled, and she was pretty shaken. Because we love her, we wanted to be with her to help out in any way we could.

Yet, here we read, Jesus purposefully delayed because He loved them. We have a really hard time wrapping our minds around that, don't we? This is an important piece of the story. Sometimes we try to apply our human understanding to God's almighty love. As a result, we don't always understand God's ways.

Pause and think. Has there been a time recently when you didn't understand God's ways? Write about that in the space below.

Two days later, Jesus tells His disciples they're going to go to Bethany in Judea because Lazarus is asleep. His disciples felt concerned. They knew that going back to Judea was dangerous for Jesus because there were many there who wanted to kill him. If Lazarus was sleeping, didn't that mean he was getting better? Then Jesus explained to them that Lazarus was dead, and that for their sakes, He was glad He wasn't there. Let's pause right there.

Imagine how confused the disciples must have felt. Jesus had told them that Lazarus's illness wouldn't end in death. But now he had died. This could have been a crisis of faith moment for them. Every crisis becomes an opportunity to re-examine your faith.

We know the end of the story, so it all makes sense to us now. But imagine how confused the disciples felt.

Read John 11:17. How long had Lazarus been dead by the time Jesus arrived?

Read John 11:21–26. Martha came running out of the house when she heard Jesus was coming. What were the first words out of her mouth? Write them here.

Read John 11:23. When tragedy strikes, our first thought is often, "If only."

Read John 11:32. Describe Mary's response to Jesus when He arrived.

Do you think Martha and Mary felt disillusioned with Jesus when He didn't come quickly? Why or why not? What evidence from the text do you have?

REFLECT

Often our perceptions of God misguide us into believing that God will always protect us and pour out blessing on us.

Author Larry Crabb wrote, "God is not committed to supporting our ministries, to preventing our divorces, to preserving our health, to straightening out our kids, to providing a livable income, to ending famine, to protecting us from agonizing problems that generate in our souls an experience that feels like death."[14]

When you first read that statement, it can feel a bit unsettling. We like to think that because God loves us, He should fix everything in our lives and make them better. But the truth is that while God wants the best for us in all things, He doesn't always answer the cries of our hearts in ways we want. He loves us completely, but He does allow suffering. When He does, we may wonder if He cares. Yes! But He calls us to trust His goodness even when life feels dark.

It's hard to understand God's ways when He seems aloof.

Think about a time in your life when you felt God was distant. In what ways did you feel disillusioned? Describe your feelings in the space below.

When Martha and Mary saw Jesus, both of them probably cried in their hearts, "If only!" I'm sure internally they wrestled with thoughts like, "If only Jesus had come sooner. If only we had called Him sooner. If only He had answered faster!"

What are your "if onlys"? List them in the space below (e.g., If only my child had not been born with that disability, or If only my husband hadn't cheated on me.).

Read Galatians 2:20. What does this verse teach us about the call to die in the life of the believer? In your journey of following Jesus, how have you had to die to self in order to live the life God is now calling you to live?

Read John 12:24. What is the promise tucked in this verse for the times in life when your dreams die?

MEMORIZE

Review John 11:25. Write it out in the space below.

PRAISE

When the Israelites were building the tabernacle, the place where God would dwell, God instructed them to build an altar on which the priest was to continuously burn fragrant incense as a blessing to the Lord (Ex. 30:1, 7–8). The incense was made through a process of crushing flowers. Similarly, the crushing of our soul produces a fragrance that rises up as a sweet aroma to God when we offer it to Him as an act of worship.

In the space below, write out a prayer of praise expressing your thanks for the times when God has allowed the crushing of your soul.

Listen to "Even When It Hurts" by Hillsong United.

WHEN YOUR DREAMS DIE, IT'S TIME FOR A RESURRECTION!

I distinctly remember a time in my husband's life when his dreams died. God had planted a vision in his heart for a very large church with many different language groups. From every outward appearance, it seemed God was moving in that direction. Steve stepped into a large church with massive potential for the kingdom. With many different language groups in the area, the location was perfect.

But soon after we started, we discovered how divided the church was: the board, the staff, and the different congregations were all on different pages. Soon the criticism began, and the hate mail was delivered to the house. After several long years, Steve resigned. His dream had died, and he felt disillusioned. I will never forget the night he came home after a long board meeting and said, "I resigned. I'm done!" We went fifteen months without a job. But here's what I know: when your dreams die, it's time for a resurrection.

In Steve's life, God began to plant a new dream. It was a bigger dream than any he had previously imagined. God planted a dream in Steve's heart for a worldwide movement of Christ followers who would seek to be the voice and hands of Jesus globally. Steve is now the CEO of a nonprofit that does just that. God has seated him in a position where he can use his visionary and leadership gifts to accomplish the task that God designed him to do.

EXPLORE

When our dreams die, it's the perfect opportunity for a resurrection of our faith. Let's return to the story in John 11.

Read John 11:17–27. Describe the emotional tone when Jesus arrived in Bethany.

Martha ran to Jesus first and cried out her "if only," as we talked about yesterday. But then Martha goes on to say, "But I know that even now God will give you whatever you ask."

What does this statement show you about Martha's faith?

Read John 11:25. It is here that Jesus makes one of His greatest *I Am* statements. Write out His *I Am* statement in the space below.

Read John 11:26.

Following His powerful *I Am* statement, Jesus asks Martha one of the most penetrating questions in the New Testament, "Do you believe this?"

The word "believe" that is used here is the Greek word *pisteúō* (Strong's #4100). It is a verb meaning "to be persuaded of." It carries the idea of analyzing the evidence and then choosing to believe based on the evidence.

When Jesus asked Martha, "Do you believe this?" He was inviting her to analyze what she had already seen and experienced with Him and form a conclusion. Martha had seen His miracles, experienced His teaching, and felt His love—now it was time to draw a conclusion. There comes a time in each of our lives when we also have to draw a conclusion about Jesus. Is He who He said He was?

Read John 11:27.

Every crisis in our lives brings us back to the question in John 11:26. Do you believe that I am the resurrection and the life? How does Martha answer? Write out her answer in the space below.

Read John 11:28–37.

Martha sends for Mary. When Mary reaches Jesus she falls at His feet weeping. Jesus was moved with compassion at the sight and sound of Mary weeping.

Read John 11:36. Circle the words of this verse in your Bible.

Imagine, the King of kings, the Lord of lords, the One who shaped the mountains and crafted the oceans, the One who put the planets and the stars in place and the One who formed intricate strands of DNA, stands there with tears streaming down His almighty face. Jesus knew the end of the story, yet He wept. What does that speak to you about Jesus?

I don't know about you, but I need a Jesus who can crawl into my suffering and sorrow. I need a Savior who weeps with me when life falls apart. I need a God who can empathize with me when life feels hopeless.

Read Hebrews 4:15. What does this verse teach you about Jesus' ability to empathize?

Read John 11:38–43. Describe the end of this story in your own words. Write your thoughts in the space below.

REFLECT

What did you learn today about how God responds when we are suffering?

Read John 11:26. Write out Jesus' question putting your name first. For example, "Becky, do you believe this?"

Write a declaration of your faith in the space below as an answer to Jesus' question.

What was the single most profound part of this story for you?

PRAISE

Listen to "Faithful God" by Gateway Worship. As you listen, reaffirm your faith by making this song your declaration of faith.

CAN HE RESURRECT YOUR MESS?

I love the writings of Andrew Murray, the missionary sent from Scotland to South Africa in the 1800s. Recently, I read about a time when Andrew felt dead due to criticism and illness. He had been pushing hard. One morning in 1895, fatigued, in pain, and smarting from attacks from critics, Andrew couldn't get out of bed. While he lay in bed before the Lord, he wrote these profound words:

In Time of Trouble Say

First, He brought me here: it is by His will I am in this strait place. In that fact I will rest.

Next, He will keep me here in His love, and give me grace to behave as His child.

Then, He will make the trial a blessing, teaching me the lessons He intends me to learn and working in me the grace He means to bestow.

Last, in His good time He can bring me out again—how and when He knows.

Let me say I am here,

By God's appointment

In His keeping

Under His training

For His time.[15]

When you feel dead and your life feels like it's one big mess, it's hard to say those words, right? Your mess can be because of your own sin, someone else's sin, or simply because unfortunate events happen. Your mess could involve your marriage; it could be problems with your kids, addictions, broken relationships, or financial struggles. In those messy moments, life seems overwhelming. Looking out over the wreckage, it's hard to believe that God can redeem and resurrect. It is in those moments that God whispers, "Do you believe?"

EXPLORE

Let's look at an Old Testament story where God asks one of His prophets that question. At the time, the people of Israel were in captivity. The situation looked hopeless for the nation of Israel, but God asks the prophet the same type of penetrating question He asked Martha. Let's take a look.

Read Ezekiel 37:1–14. As Ezekiel stands looking at the Valley of Dry Bones, what is the question God asks him? How is this question similar to the one Jesus asked Martha in John 11:26?

Ezekiel stood there looking over the wreckage and stammered, "Sovereign Lord, you alone know!" What a great answer! Imagine, an entire valley filled with dried-up bones. I wonder if Ezekiel thought, "Lord, they look pretty dead to me!" The imagery of the scene is symbolic of Israel being completely without hope. Sometimes circumstances in our lives lead us to believe that there is no hope. But that is not true.

The Lord tells Ezekiel to speak to the bones and declare that the Lord Himself will breathe new life into those bones and that they will come alive once again.

Read Ezekiel 37:9–10.

Next, the Lord tells Ezekiel to call for the breath of God's Spirit to breathe life into the bones so they are fully alive and ready to become a vast army. Similarly, when our dreams die, God invites us to look at the wreckage of our broken dreams, and He whispers in our ears, "Do you believe I can resurrect this mess?"

- Can I resurrect your broken marriage?
- Can I resurrect your shattered dreams?
- Can I resurrect your drained finances?
- Can I resurrect your grave failures?
- Can I resurrect your ruins and rebuild something beautiful?

Read Ezekiel 37:12. What is the promise that God makes to Ezekiel concerning His ability to give life? How does this promise tie into the promise of Jesus being the resurrection and the life?

The correlation between Ezekiel and the resurrection of dry bones and the raising of Lazarus is striking. The great sovereign I Am of the Old Testament who can raise dry bones into a living army is the same great I Am of the New Testament who can raise a man who has been dead for four days back to life. The implication for us is that death no longer has the final word. Jesus Christ, the great I Am, has conquered death eternally. For you and me, this is a message of incredible hope! Jesus is able not only to resurrect dry bones and dead bodies, but He has absolute authority and ability to resurrect your mess.

Read 1 Corinthians 15:54–58. Make a list of the reasons you have hope according to these verses.

REFLECT

Think about a situation in your life that feels hopeless. Write about that situation in the space below.

Like Ezekiel prophesied over the dry bones and declared God's power over the dead bones, write out a prayer declaring God's power and goodness over your situation.

MEMORIZE

Make a list of broken dreams in your life. With a red marker, write over the whole list the words of John 11:25.

PRAISE

Listen to "Get Your Hopes Up" by Josh Baldwin. As you listen, praise Jesus for all the reasons He gives you hope.

WEEK 5 | DAY 5

THE SAME POWER THAT RESURRECTED JESUS NOW LIVES IN YOU

The bottom line is that empowerment by God's Spirit
is a necessity for success.
Supernatural acts require supernatural equipping.
—Priscilla Shirer

Remember the story at the beginning of this week about Dr. John Slater? What gave him the faith to pray the prayer that saved both the life of the mother and the child? What allowed him to speak the gospel message clearly in the language of the tribe? It was a deep understanding that the same power that raised Lazarus from the dead and the same power that raised Jesus from the dead now lived in him!

Friend, if you grow to fully understand that power is yours through Christ, you will be unstoppable in God's kingdom. Self-doubt and fear will no longer hold you back. Despair over broken dreams will no longer paralyze you; instead, you will gain a growing awareness that though life might not be what you expected, Jesus will resurrect your mess, whatever it is. He is more than able to bring new life where dry bones formerly lay. And all the power that you need to face your trials dwells in you as Christ dwells in you. Wow! Talk about hope. There it is. This is the promise of the One who is the resurrection and the life.

My prayer for you as we close out this week echoes the prayer of the apostle Paul for the believers living in Ephesus.

EXPLORE

Read Ephesians 1:15–23.

The apostle Paul prayed that the Ephesian believers would be given the Spirit of wisdom and revelation so that they would grow deeper in their understanding of the power of Christ. He prayed that their eyes would be opened so that they would gain a deeper understanding of the hope available to them and the incomparably great power that they had access to. Paul goes on to describe that power.

Write your own description of the power that raised Jesus from the dead.

How does Christ's resurrection power fuel you with hope?

Read Ephesians 1:20–22. Describe the power and authority Jesus Christ now has because He has conquered death.

Read Romans 8:9–11. What do these verses teach you about Christ's indwelling power?

According to these verses, what part does the Holy Spirit play in empowering you?

The Holy Spirit is the third person of the Trinity. According to John 14:26, Jesus left us the Holy Spirit to indwell us as our power source.

Read Luke 24:49. Why did Jesus tell the disciples to wait in the city after He left and ascended to heaven?

Here are a few truths about the Holy Spirit.

The Holy Spirit exalts Jesus Christ. (John 12:32)

The Holy Spirit is called the Spirit of truth. (John 14:17)

The Holy Spirit indwells every believer. (John 14:17–18)

The Holy Spirit is a counselor who reminds us of what Jesus has said. (John 14:26)

The Holy Spirit communicates with us. (John 15:26, 16:7–11)

The Holy Spirit empowers us. (Rom. 8:9–11)

The Holy Spirit gifts us to serve the body of Christ more effectively. (1 Cor. 12:4–11)

REFLECT

Read Galatians 5:22–26. If these character traits are the fruit of the Spirit living through us, what do you think is our part in developing these character traits, and what do you think is the Holy Spirit's part?

How would your life look different if you truly believed that the power of Christ resided in you?

What was one key principle you learned this week about the Holy Spirit?

If Jesus were to ask you "Do you believe this?", how would you answer?

How has your faith grown this past week as you studied Jesus as the Resurrection and the Life?

MEMORIZE

Write out John 11:25 from memory in the space below.

PRAISE

Listen to "Same Power" by Jeremy Camp. As you listen, praise God that His resurrection power lives in you and is available to you!

WEEK SIX

do you want to get well?

When Jesus saw him lying there and learned that
he had been in this condition for a long time, he asked him,
"Do you want to get well?"

JOHN 5:6

I AM THE WAY, THE TRUTH, AND THE LIFE

Jesus answered, "I am the way and the truth and the life. No one
comes to the Father except through me."

JOHN 14:6

WEEK 6 | DAY 1

DO YOU WANT TO GET WELL?

JOHN 5:6

The work of restoration cannot begin until the problem is fully faced.
—Dan B. Allender

I remember a pivotal moment in my life when I felt the Holy Spirit speak directly to my soul, asking, "Becky. . ."

Do you want to get well?

Honestly, I paused and considered my answer carefully.

Getting well for me meant admitting the truth about what had happened in my childhood and agreeing to go to a Christian therapist for some godly counseling. I just wasn't sure I was up for that type of adventure. My excuses were plenty: I'm a pastor's wife. Everyone knows. Pastors' wives don't go for counseling. Counseling costs too much. We would never be able to afford therapy.

The biggest excuse by far was, "What will people think?"

But as a child of God, my life was no longer my own. When I decided to follow Jesus, I gave up the rights to my own life. When Jesus showed me that the way to healing included counseling, I obeyed.

Excuses are common when God asks such a penetrating question. Certainly, the man at the pool of Bethesda was no exception. He had lived with his infirmity for so long that he had become comfortable with being lame. It was his normal.

EXPLORE

Read John 5:1–18.

I visited the pool of Bethesda a few years ago while traveling in Israel. The pool was located directly over some underground springs of water. When the water bubbled up from the spring, people thought an angel was stirring the water and that if they rolled in they would be healed. Believing for a miracle, the lame man lay there waiting. But he never quite made it into the pool. Victimized by unfortunate circumstances, he was left crippled.

Describe the scene in these verses in your own words.

How long had the man been an invalid?

I sympathize with this man. A few years ago, I broke my ankle. I had to wear a cast for a few weeks, hobbled around on crutches, graduated to a walking boot, and finally upgraded to an ankle stabilizer. I looked lame. I walked lame. I felt lame. But I was lame only for a summer. This man had been lame for a long time.

It's easy when we've experienced unfortunate events to settle into "lame thinking." Lame thinkers feel victimized. Lame thinkers feel they have no options in life. Lame thinkers imagine that their circumstances will likely never change. As I see it, lame thinking falls into two categories: self-limiting beliefs and God-limiting beliefs.

Fill in the chart below with some common self-limiting beliefs and God-limiting beliefs:

SELF-LIMITING BELIEFS	GOD-LIMITING BELIEFS
1.	
2.	
3.	
4.	
5.	
6.	
7.	

Do you think this man struggled with lame thinking? Why or why not? What evidence do you have?

All of us have experienced hurt and unfortunate events. How have the hurts of your past caused you to settle for lame thinking?

Read John 5:2. Circle the word "Bethesda," which means outpouring. In the margin of your Bible write the word "outpouring." Why might that word "outpouring" be significant to the story?

Read the question Jesus asks in John 5:6 again. Circle the word "well." In the Greek, the word "well" means "sound, whole, healthy" (Strong's #5199). In your life, what would it look like to be made whole?

In order to be made whole, what addictions, insecurities, hurts, or hang-ups might you need to surrender?

Read John 5:8–9. Why do you think Jesus asked the man to pick up his mat when He commanded Him to walk? How did the lame man act by faith in response to Jesus' question and command?

REFLECT

How do self-limiting beliefs and God-limiting beliefs cripple you spiritually?

In our lives, we need a fresh outpouring of the Holy Spirit's presence and power to deepen our faith and make us whole. What might an outpouring look like in your life?

If Jesus were to ask you, "Do you want to get well?", what areas of your life might make you hesitate to answer yes?

PRAISE

Write out a prayer of praise thanking Christ that He came to show you the way to wholeness.

Listen to "Broken Vessels" (Amazing Grace) by Hillsong Worship. Praise Jesus that He is not intimidated by your brokenness. On the contrary, He came for broken people like you.

FINDING YOUR WAY

When Jesus asks a question like, "Do you want to get well?" He doesn't leave us hanging. He shows us the way, because He is the way. In fact, He emphatically answers.

Do you want to get well?
I Am **the Way, the Truth, and the Life**

He claimed to be the only complete resource for becoming whole. What does that mean? If it feels a bit confusing, don't worry, you're not alone.

The disciples felt confused as well. Jesus was talking about leaving. They had just had an intimate dinner with Him when He began saying some disturbing things about leaving and dying. When Peter asked where He was going, Jesus responded that where He was going they couldn't go until later (John 13:36). Where was He going? And why couldn't they follow? In gentleness, Jesus began addressing the deep concerns of their anxious hearts.

EXPLORE

Read John 14:1–7. Jesus began by saying to the disciples, "Do not let your hearts be troubled." Describe a "troubled heart" in your own words.

From a human perspective, the disciples had every reason to feel troubled. What do you think Jesus' tone was like? Do you think He was rebuking them for having troubled hearts, or do you think He was offering comfort?

Read John 14:1.

Jesus went on to say, "You believe in God; believe also in me." There's the word "believe" again.

Circle the word "believe" in your Bible. Once again, write out the definition in your own words in the space below. What strategic choices can a person make to cultivate belief in Jesus?

When your heart is troubled, what does it look like to put your faith into action?

Read John 14:2.

Jesus went on to explain to the disciples that after His death and resurrection He would be leaving to prepare a place for them in His Father's house.

What do you think His "Father's house" refers to?

Read 1 John 3:2. What does this verse teach about your ultimate wholeness?

Read John 14:3–4. What is the promise found there?

At this point in the conversation, Thomas, completely baffled, cried out the question the other disciples were likely thinking but embarrassed to voice: "Lord, we don't know where you're going, so how can we know the way?"

In response, Jesus made one of the boldest statements found in the Bible. It can be a tripping point for many today too. In our post-modern generation, it's not politically correct to make such a bold and exclusive statement. But Jesus wasn't one to worry about being politically correct.

Jesus said boldly, emphatically, categorically, "I am the way and the truth and the life. No one comes to the Father except through me." Bam! Not exactly inclusive or sensitive to people of other faiths. Let's break it down and take a deeper look.

The English language does not do justice to the power behind this statement of Jesus. In Greek it would read, "I am the way because I am the truth and because I am the life. I am the way to the Father because I am the true manifestation or revelation of the Father."[16]

Circle in your Bible the definite article "the" in "I am the way."

Notice Jesus didn't say, I'm one of the ways. Or I'm a way. No. He said, I am *the* way!

Jesus is the only way to:

- Peace with God the Father
- Forgiveness for our sins and shortcomings
- Emotional and spiritual healing
- Freedom from addiction and anxiety

Not only is He "The Way," but He also shows us the way to become all He's created us to be and to find healing and wholeness in Him.

Look up each of the verses listed below. Next to each verse complete the sentence: Jesus is the way to _____.

1 Corinthians 6:20

Isaiah 43:4

Isaiah 41:10

Mark 6:31

Hebrews 10:22

1 John 1:9

REFLECT

How does it affect your faith to realize the strength and boldness behind Jesus' statement "I am the way"?

After studying Jesus as the Way, what would you say to someone who said, "Well, Jesus works for you, but I believe. . . ."

What is God speaking to you about Jesus being the Way to your personal wholeness?

MEMORIZE

Write out the words to John 14:6. This might be one of the most important verses you memorize in this study!

PRAISE

Listen to "Only Jesus" by Brian Johnson. As you listen, worship Jesus Christ as the only way to peace with God and the only way to wholeness in your life.

FACE TO FACE WITH TRUTH

Remember, we started our week with the question Jesus asked the lame man, "Do you want to get well?" Today, He asks you the same question. The path to becoming whole begins when you put your faith in Jesus as the way, but the path doesn't end there. Jesus continued His startling statement by saying, "and the truth" (John 14:6).

We are living in a culture that teaches that truth is relative. The narrative goes something like this: "Your truth might not be my truth. My truth might not be your truth." As a result, many are left wondering—if Jesus claims to be absolute truth and to follow Him means to believe that He is the ONLY way to God, does that make a person a bigot? Or does it make you judgmental? Ah, makes you squirm, doesn't it? Our society has taught us that "I don't have a right to impose my truth on you, and you don't have the right to impose your truth on me."

Present-day evangelicalism is now wrestling with the gravity of Jesus' bold statement. What are the implications as far as Christ's absolute authority, and how urgent is the gospel? Where you land on this issue is important. Therefore, it's a good moment to pause and pray.

May I invite you? The ramifications of this statement, "I am the truth," are so life-changing that you need to pause and pray. Ask the Holy Spirit to open your heart to a deeper understanding of Jesus' identity and its significance for your life. Then, after you've prayed, open your Bible to John 14.

Read John 14:1–7. Describe the tone behind Jesus' statement, "I am the truth."

Read John 14:7. What does this verse teach you about the identity of Jesus?

Read the following verses, and write a concluding statement about Jesus' identity:

Matthew 14:32–33

John 10:30–31

John 8:57–59

Colossians 1:15–17

Either Christ was truly God or He was an imposter. What evidence do you have that Jesus Christ really was God?

Read Mark 8:31; Mark 16:5–7; Luke 23:44–47; Luke 24:1–12; and 1 Corinthians 15:6. If Jesus truly is God, what does that say about His authority?

REFLECT

Satan is called the father of lies (John 8:44). He loves to get us tangled up in lies. As the truth, Jesus came to save us from both the deceiver and deception. In your quest for wholeness, truth is essential! And even though we value truth, it's easy to fall for Satan's tricks and even to deceive ourselves. Think about it. How often have you heard the following statements?

- I'm not addicted. I'm in control; I can stop whenever I want.
- I'll never be victorious! I've struggled with this _____ for too long. I'm going to just give up.
- I can't change. I was born this way, and God wants me to be happy.
- I'm not as bad as other people.

Most of us are pretty good at protecting ourselves. What are some of the lies you've told yourself?

Read John 8:31–32, 36. What do these verses speak to you about the correlation between truth and freedom?

The first step toward finding wholeness and freedom is admitting the truth. Spend a few moments quietly praying. Ask the Holy Spirit to search your heart and show you any area where you may be deceiving yourself. Ask Him to give you the courage to face the truth and find freedom.

Write your prayer in the space below.

MEMORIZE

Review John 14:6.

PRAISE

Listen to "Resurrecting" by Elevation Worship. As you listen, spend time praising God that the lies that have held you captive in the past are being broken by Christ's truth. Praise God that in Christ you are set free.

THE LIFE YOU'VE ALWAYS WANTED

Every time Steve and I have a new grandchild, I am astounded by the miracle and beauty of new life. Precious little ones come into the world, gasp for their first breath, let out their first cry, and inspire me to simply worship the God of life who gives, renews, and sustains life. When I hold a new grandchild for the first time and gaze deeply into their little eyes and feel the grip of their tiny hand grasping my finger, I wonder, how could anyone not believe in God, the giver of life? It's such a miracle!

I think the apostle John felt similarly because the theme of "life" permeates his gospel. It is a word that Jesus used often. He described abundant life, new life, and eternal life.

After Jesus claimed to be the way and the truth, He then went on to claim He was "the life" (John 14:6). He was and is the essence of life, the source of life, the sustainer of life, and the provider of abundant life. The life you've always wanted is found in Him!

EXPLORE

Read each of the following verses. Underline the word *life* in each
verse, then write down one takeaway about life from each verse.

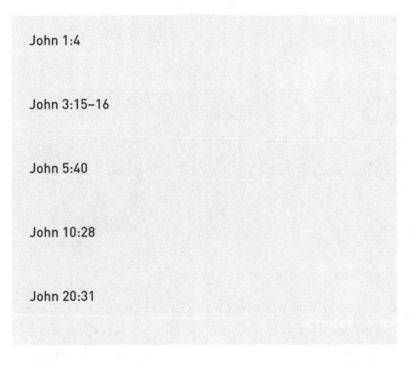

John 1:4

John 3:15–16

John 5:40

John 10:28

John 20:31

Read John 10:10. According to this verse, why did Jesus come? How
would you describe "the full life"?

Read Colossians 1:15–18. What do these verses tell you about Jesus as the source of life?

Read Luke 20:2. The authority of Jesus was and is continually questioned. How would you answer the question that the Pharisees asked Jesus, "Who gave you this authority?"

Jesus offered full life to the lame man who lay by the pool of Bethesda. Not only did He heal him physically in John 5:8–9, but Jesus also reminded the man that even though he had been healed physically, he needed to be healed spiritually to live the rich life that God had for him (John 5:14–15).

Read Galatians 2:20. What does a person need to exchange in order to receive the life that Christ offers? What does it mean to you personally to be crucified with Christ?

REFLECT

Read Colossians 2:6–7. What do these verses teach you about your new life in Christ?

As you reflect on your new life, what changes have you experienced?

What has been the biggest contribution to your personal growth as you've matured in your new life?

PRAISE

Colossians 2:7 instructs us to be "overflowing with thankfulness" because of our new life in Christ.

Make a thankful list in the space below for all the ways Christ has changed your life.

WEEK 6 | DAY 5

THE IMPLICATIONS OF YOUR NEW LIFE

We've covered a lot of ground this week, haven't we? Let's go back to the lame man lying by the pool. Remember, "Bethesda" means outpouring. I pray that this week you've experienced an outpouring of the Holy Spirit reawakening your heart to the authority, power, and majesty of Jesus Christ. I pray that you've experienced an outpouring of His love and forgiveness over your life.

Remember the question that Jesus asked the lame man? "Do you want to get well?" Let's read that passage again, but this time, put yourself in the story. Imagine you are the lame man and The Great I Am, the Way, the Truth and the Life, stands before you and asks, "My beloved child, do you want to get well?"

EXPLORE

Read John 5:1–8.

I believe Jesus had the man pick up his mat so that the lame man would understand, once he walked, there was no going back. In your life, once Jesus shows you the way, brings you face to face with Himself as the truth, and gives you new life—*there's no going back!*

How do we keep from going back to the old patterns from which Christ has set us free? How do we live as those who have found new life in Christ? To answer those questions, let's turn to the book of Colossians.

Read Colossians 3:1–4. Answer the following questions:

What does it look like to set your mind and heart on Christ's desires?

What does it mean to you that you died and your life is now hidden in Christ?

Circle the phrase in verse 4 that says "When Christ, who is your life." Pause and reflect: what are the implications of Christ being your life?

Write some statements in the space below that finish the phrase, "Because Christ is my life, _____." Include thoughts about how Christ being your life shapes your priorities (e.g., how you spend your time and money and where you place your focus).

Read Colossians 3:5. What does it look like for you to put to death old habits that prevent you from living the life Christ has for you?

Read Colossians 3:12–14. List the character traits that are to be a part of your new life in Christ.

How might forgiving others be one way Jesus plans for you to find wholeness?

REFLECT

How has your answer to the question "Who do you say that I am?" been strengthened this week?

What did God speak to you this week? Where is God calling you to obey Him?

PRAISE

Listen to "Beautiful Surrender" by Jonathan and Melissa Helser. As you listen, praise God that you can trust Him and surrender to Him.

can you add to your life by worrying?

"Can any one of you by worrying add a single hour to your life?"

MATTHEW 6:27

"Who of you by worrying can add a single hour to your life?"

LUKE 12:25

I AM THE VINE

"I am the vine; you are the branches. If you remain in me and I in you, you will bear much fruit; apart from me you can do nothing."

JOHN 15:5

WEEK 7 | DAY 1

CAN YOU ADD TO YOUR LIFE BY WORRYING?

MATTHEW 6:27, LUKE 12:25

> *Worry doesn't empty tomorrow of its sorrow,*
> *it empties today of its strength.*
> —Linda Dillow

For as far back as I can remember, worry and anxiety have been a part of my journey. Growing up, I was a worried little kid. I worried about all sorts of things, including getting good grades, making enough friends, playing the piano well, and acting on the burden for my little friends to know Jesus. I'm pretty sure I was neurotic.

I remember lying in bed at night praying, "Jesus, make me brave enough to suffer for you." Who prays that as a little kid? I didn't want to worry. But I did. To make matters worse, I heard lots of sermons on how "worry was a sin." That compounded my problem. It was a vicious cycle that I simply couldn't break.

My worries followed me right into adulthood. The question, "what if" terrified me: What if Steve dies and I am left to finish raising the kids? What if something bad happens to my kids? What if God calls me to be persecuted for Him and I crumble under pressure? What if I can't do the tasks God calls me to do? The more I worried, the more I felt guilty, and the more I felt guilty, the more I worried. The bottom line, I felt inadequate to be the woman God had called me to be.

One day the Lord spoke to me in His quiet whisper, saying, "Becky, you are living through nightmares I never intended you to live through . . ."

Can you add to your life by worrying?

Good question!

I remember whispering back, "Uh. . . no, but, I don't know how to stop or contain these worries. I need you to show me how, Lord Jesus. I want to live boldly and confidently for you; I simply don't know how." Jesus answered that prayer. Gradually, ever so gradually, He has helped me to find freedom, function in boldness, and contain my anxiety. Please notice, I didn't say I became worry free.

What Jesus taught me was how to surrender my worries to Him. He taught me that rather than obsessing about what could happen, I should obsess about Him. Through the help of His Spirit, I learned to step past my anxiety.

Gradually, I began to practice three key principles that changed my life: admit, abide, and adore. As we move through this week, we're going to look at each of those principles in depth.

ADMIT

Let's get real, okay? Worry and anxiety threaten almost every woman I know. Some say they don't worry, but then when I am listening to them in conversations, I hear otherwise.

If left unchecked, worry and anxiety:

- Cripple our creativity
- Derail our decision making
- Rob our sleep
- Give us stomach ulcers
- Plague our parenting journey
- Mess with our marriages
- Stifle our spiritual growth

I can feel you groaning. Now I've just given you more to worry about, right?

What in the world are we supposed to do? Guilt surely doesn't help. Covering up and denying our worry doesn't help. I've got good news for you. This week I'm going to give you some tangible steps to contain your worries.

Let's begin by taking a look at the question Jesus asked the disciples in Matthew 6:27.

EXPLORE

Read Matthew 6:25–27.

This section of Scripture is part of what Bible scholars call the Sermon on the Mount. It is the teaching that Christ did on the side of a hill where thousands gathered to hear Him. It is recorded for us in Matthew 5–7. For our purposes we're going to focus on Matthew 6:25–27. In these verses, Jesus asks three great questions. But before we look at those questions, let's take a look at the section that comes before.

Read Matthew 6:19–24. Why do you think Jesus introduced His thoughts on worry by talking about money?

What do you think Jesus meant when He said that you can't serve God and money? How does money become our master when we worry about our financial well-being?

Anything we obsess about ultimately becomes our master!

THREE GREAT QUESTIONS

Matthew 6:25 begins with the word "Therefore." Whenever you see the word "therefore" in Scripture, you need to look back on what's previously been said in order to understand what will be said next. In other words, it was as if Jesus was saying, "In light of what I've just taught you concerning money, don't worry!"

Circle the word "worry" in your Bible.

The word "worry" that's used here is the Greek word *merimnáō* (Strong's #3309). The root of that word is *merizo*, which means "to divide into parts." The word carries the idea of a distraction, a pre-occupation with things that cause anxiety, stress, and pressure. That's exactly what worry does to us, doesn't it? It causes us to be distracted from the things God wants us focused on, and it creates a stressed-out feeling in our bodies. As a result, we become preoccupied with problems rather than the Problem Solver.

To help us untangle ourselves from worry, Jesus asked three great questions. Take a look at each question. Beneath each one, write what you think the point is behind the question and what the implication is for your life.

1. Is not life more than food and the body more than clothes?

2. Are you not much more valuable than they?

3. Can any one of you by worrying add a single hour to your life?

In my own journey to contain my worry and anxiety, I admitted I had a problem, and I analyzed the futility of worrying. I began to ask myself, "How is worrying about this helping me?" The answer, of course, was that it wasn't helping me at all. Instead, obsessing about what might go wrong was adding to the stress and pressure I already felt in life. It was putting me in bondage to worry. Once I realized that, I began to consider what it meant to abide in Christ. Before we look at abiding, I want you to take a few moments and reflect on how worry has impacted you.

REFLECT

Make a list of the things you most often worry about. (Please be honest. No one is going to read your answers except you.) Next to each worry, write what you think Jesus might say about that worry.

How much do you think you're worth to God?

Read the following verses. Next to each one, write how you can know you are of great value to God.

Isaiah 49:15

Jeremiah 31:3

Romans 5:8

1 Peter 1:18–19

In my journey to overcome worry and anxiety, understanding my position in Christ helped to quiet the worry and anxiety in my heart. As I internalized Jesus as the vine, I realized I only had to abide in Him, and He would empower me to do anything He called me to do and empower me to face anything He called me to face. Tomorrow, join me in the vineyard as we figure out who's who and what's what and then we'll delve into what it means to abide. But first, spend a few minutes praising God that He invites us to give our worries to Him.

PRAISE

Listen to "I Will Look Up" by Elevation Worship. As you listen, praise God that He cares for you and carries your worries.

WHO'S WHO AND WHAT'S WHAT IN THE VINEYARD?

After I was willing to admit that I had a problem with worry, I began to consider what it looked like to abide in Christ. There is no better place to figure out abiding than John 15 where Jesus gave the answer to His question about worry.

> Can you add to your life by worrying?
> *I Am* the Vine

Before we consider what it means to abide, let's look at the background and consider who's who and what's what in the vineyard.

Jesus was preparing the disciples for His imminent departure, and they were feeling worried. Who could blame them? Jesus was using phrases like "dying" and "leaving soon." It all felt confusing and worrisome to the disciples. But Jesus knew He had to prepare them because soon He would face the cross, and after His resurrection He would be leaving them to take His rightful place beside the Father.

To add stress upon stress, He was about to leave them with an impossible task: "Go and make disciples of all nations, baptizing them in the name of the Father and of the Son and of the Holy Spirit" (Matt. 28:19). It's as if Jesus was preparing to say, "No big deal, guys, just go change the entire world!"

What was Jesus thinking? Certainly He could have come up with a better team—such an important task left to such an uneducated and unpolished group of fishermen. A more unqualified group would be hard to imagine. James and John argued over who was the greatest. Peter consistently put his foot in his mouth. Thomas wrestled with doubt. How could this rag-tag group be transformed into preachers, leaders, and writers who would change the world and found the early church?

Jesus knew panic would envelope them if He didn't give them a clear picture of their position in Him. So Jesus chose an illustration the disciples would understand: a grapevine. One of the things I love most about Jesus is His teaching style. The simple illustrations He used to make a point were profound. Grapevines were very familiar to the disciples. They were central to Israel's agriculture and economy.

FUN FACTS ABOUT GRAPES

In order for you to better understand Jesus' message on the correlation between abiding and fruitfulness, let me give you some fun facts about grapes and how they're grown.

- Grapes are widely grown all over the world.
- Even today, if you travel in Israel, you'll see grapevines. They continue to be an important part of Israel's economy.
- The grapevine is Israel's national emblem.
- The vine is only as good as its roots.
- Individual branches are often grafted into vines that are productive.
- Grapevines require loving care. They must be watered, fertilized, and pruned in order to flourish.
- New plants are pruned every three to five years before they are even allowed to produce a crop of grapes.[17]
- Grapevines are productive and yield as much as eighty pounds of grapes in a single season.

Understanding those facts helps us to realize that Jesus was saying to the disciples, "Fruitfulness is my plan for your life!" The key was going to be their abiding in Him.

EXPLORE

Read John 15:1–5.

Look at the list below. Identify who/what fulfills each role and how according to John 15.

Who's the Vine?

Who's the Gardener?

Who are the branches?

What's the fruit?

Read John 15:5. Circle in your Bible the statement in verse 5 that says "I am the vine; you are the branches." What is the relationship between the branch and the vine? What does that say about your relationship with Jesus?

Read Isaiah 4:2. How does this prophecy point to the coming of Jesus Christ?

Read John 15:4. Circle the phrase "in me" in your Bible. What does this verse say about our position in Christ?

Read John 15:5. What is the promise in this verse for those who remain in Christ?

REFLECT

Read 2 Corinthians 5:17. What does this verse teach you about your position in Christ?

Read Ephesians 2:10.

When you are "in Christ," what is the natural result as far as fruitfulness and good works? What are the good works that you feel God has specifically called you to do? List them below.

PRAISE

Listen to "In Christ Alone" by Kristian Stanfill. As you listen, praise God that by simply abiding in Christ, you will be able to live a fruitful life.

WHAT DOES IT LOOK LIKE TO ABIDE?

Remember, I stated at the beginning of this week that I had to learn how to admit, abide, and adore. Today, we're going to explore abiding. Let's get down to the nitty-gritty of what it means to abide, especially if you struggle with worry.

Of all the things I worried about, near the top was failing. I didn't want my life to not count for anything. Unproductivity seemed right up there with insignificance. I wanted to change the world for Jesus, but what if I failed? What if I never accomplished anything of any eternal value? I needed to shift my attitude from achieving to abiding.

ABIDE

One summer, exhausted from my own striving, I printed out John 15 in double-spaced format. All summer, I read and re-read the passage. I circled phrases, highlighted thoughts, and wrote notes all over my printout. I memorized and meditated. I needed to figure out what exactly it meant to abide.

EXPLORE

Read through John 15. Every time you read the word "remain" or "abide" (depending on whether you are using the NIV or ESV version), underline it. Count how many times the word is used.

The word "remain" in the Greek means "to stay, abide or remain" (Strong's #3306). It carries the idea of being with someone. Abiding is about relationship. When we abide in Christ, the pressure to perform is off. We focus on abiding rather than worrying about achieving.

What do you think it looks like to abide?

Fill in the area below listing the differences between someone who is worried about achieving and someone simply focused on abiding.

Achiever	vs.	Abider

Read Philippians 2:13. What does this verse teach you about the difference between achieving and abiding?

Read John 15:5–11. When we abide, we purposefully remain close to Christ. We cultivate a sense of His presence in our lives so that we are reminded that He does the work, we only have to remain. List the benefits of abiding that you see in the verses.

Read John 15:14–15. What is the correlation between abiding in Christ and loving others?

Read John 15:16–17. How does abiding affect our prayer lives?

REFLECT

Do you consider yourself more of an achiever or an abider? Why?

Our culture drives us to succeed. But those who are worried about achieving feel driven to accomplish something worthwhile in order to be of value.

In your life, how have you wrestled with the drive to achieve?

The problem is, our lives are busy, full, hectic, and often frazzled. How in the world do we cultivate ongoing communion with God?

Write down your ideas in the space below.

We can cultivate communion with God in many different ways: prayer, Bible reading, listening to worship music, or taking a walk in nature.

In what ways do you intentionally connect with God every day? Where do you most feel His presence?

PRAISE

Jesus promises His presence with us, but He loves to hear the longing of His child's heart for His presence. Worship and praise Jesus as one who abides with you, and ask Him to raise your awareness of His presence in your life today.

Listen to "Here as in Heaven" by Elevation Worship. As you listen, praise Jesus Christ that His indwelling Spirit is with you 24/7. At times, we are more aware and more in sync with the presence and power of the Spirit. As you worship, ask the Lord for deeper understanding of the power of His Spirit in your life. This is a prayer that the Lord delights to answer!

FIGURING OUT FRUITFULNESS

*The essential idea of fruit
is that it is the silent, natural, restful produce of our inner life.*
—Andrew Murray

During the summer that I studied John 15, I recorded my observations, thoughts, and feelings, and I made a startling discovery: *the branch was never stressed out or worried!*

Pause and think about that. Have you ever seen a stressed-out branch? No, of course not. The branch simply rests and remains in the vine. That seems to be the key to fruitfulness. It's as if Jesus says, "Don't worry about being fruitful or being more productive. You just stay close and let me do the work!"

EXPLORE

Read all of John 15. Using a highlighter, highlight every instance of the words "fruit," "fruitful," or "fruitfulness" in this passage. What do your highlights show you about the priority God places on fruitful living?

Read John 15:5–6. When you think of fruitfulness, what comes to mind?

Read the following verses and record your ideas about fruitfulness.

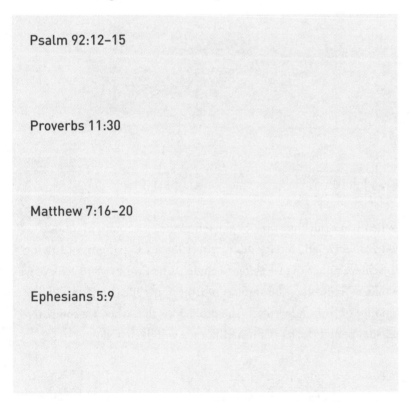

Psalm 92:12–15

Proverbs 11:30

Matthew 7:16–20

Ephesians 5:9

There are two kinds of fruit in the life of the believer: internal and external.

Read Galatians 5:22–25. What do these verses teach you about internal fruit? What part does the Holy Spirit play in the internal fruit production?

Read Ephesians 2:10. What does this verse teach you about external fruit?

Read John 15:5. Underline the phrase "much fruit."

When you read "much fruit," the temptation to compare yourself with others might surface. It's easy to fall back to patterns of striving to achieve rather than seeking to abide. When we strive to achieve we wonder, "How does the amount of fruit in my life compare with the amount of fruit in her life?" The problem is that when we compare, self-doubt and the fear of insignificance will likely follow.

According to John 15:5, what is God's part, and what is your part in bearing much fruit?

Pruning is good for every vineyard. When the gardener prunes, the branches of the vine produce more fruit. Let's take a deeper look so that we understand this more clearly.

WHAT'S UP WITH THE PRUNING?

Read John 15:2, 6.

When you read that the gardener "cuts off" (*airei*) the branches not bearing fruit and prunes (*kathairei*) the branch that does bear fruit, those words might lead you to believe that if you don't measure up, God's going to cut you off. I don't believe that's true.

In both verses 2 and 6, the branches refer to those who are followers of Jesus. They are people who have put their faith and trust in Jesus Christ to save them, but they've lost their close connection with the vine. As a result, they're not bearing fruit. There are two views on what vine-dressing means in this case:

1. Some biblical scholars believe that "fire" and "burned" mentioned in verse 6 symbolize "uselessness" of the branches that don't abide in Christ, and as a result, they fall under "divine discipline now and reproof at the future evaluation of believers."[18]

2. Other biblical scholars believe a better translation of *airei* would be "take up" or "lift up."[19] This speaks to sanctification, or the process of making a believer more like Jesus Christ. Though this view is less popular among biblical scholars, I believe it is more accurate as it reflects the vine-growing culture of Israel and fits with the grace-offering disposition of Jesus that I see in the rest of the gospels.

Romans 8:1 teaches us that there is no condemnation for those who have put their faith and trust in Jesus Christ. While God disciplines us, it is done without condemnation for the purpose of our sanctification and our becoming more like Jesus Christ. As I've studied this passage, I believe that the second meaning of the verb *airei*, to "take up" or "lift up," better fits the rest of Christ's teaching. *The Moody Bible Commentary* says "springtime (the time of the upper room message and Jesus' death) was the season to 'lift up' fruitless branches from the ground to encourage productivity."[20] This is a great image of what I believe Jesus was referring to when He taught this truth about sanctification.

In either case, God's desire for you is to become more like His Son, Jesus Christ, and to live a life abundant in fruit. What specifically does pruning look like? It might come in the form of difficulty or hardship. In those times, we will press more deeply into Jesus, and our close connection with Him will be reestablished.

The Gardener also prunes those whose lives are fruitful. Why? Pruning cuts branches back to their place of connection and allows the connection to become enlarged. This enlargement enables more life-giving sap to pour through the branch, resulting in more fruit. For the vine to produce "much fruit," the inner life of the branch must be expanded.

The only way to allow that deep connection with God to expand is by abiding and cooperating with God's pruning in your life.

How can you cooperate with God's pruning process in your life?

Read John 15:16. How does the fact that God has chosen you to bear fruit free you from worry?

I love author Heather Holleman's thoughts on fruitfulness: "Do you realize what this means? Do you understand the far-reaching, all-consuming implications of this for someone like me who's been in bondage to achievement all her life? It means that I'm free. . . I stop the frenzied clamoring to achieve because Jesus has already chosen and designed the particular good works for my life."[21]

Read John 14:15–17 and John 15:26. How does the indwelling Holy Spirit produce fruit in our lives?

REFLECT

When you consider that God has chosen you to bear fruit, how does that impact your self-esteem?

When you think of fruit bearing, do you think it's easier to bear external fruit or internal fruit? Why?

Pruning invites us to surrender to the Gardener, and it often cuts to the core of our identity. This is because we tend to derive our identity from things we greatly value: our roles, our jobs, our kids, our spouse, or our possessions. All of these are good things; it's just that God wants your identity rooted deeply in Christ.

When your life becomes deeply rooted in Christ, you worry less because you discover all that you need is found in Him. Think about a time in your life where God allowed difficult circumstances to help reshape your identity. What did that season look like? How did it result in your identity being more firmly rooted in Christ?

PRAISE

When we intentionally cultivate an attitude of adoration toward Jesus Christ, His Spirit quiets our anxiety and our striving to achieve. Instead, the fruit of Christ-likeness gradually begins to grow in our lives.

Listen to "Here I Bow" by Jenn Johnson. As you listen, surrender every worry and any anxiety you might have over bearing fruit.

LIVING A FREE AND FRUITFUL LIFE

The deeper our roots go in Christ, the more we are able to live free from our worries and be fruitful in the power of His Holy Spirit. First we admit we have a problem with worry. Then we learn to abide and gradually, as we focus on abiding in Christ, we naturally begin adoring Him. As we adore Him, He replaces anxiety with calm, fear with faith, and dread with boldness. We slowly learn that as the branch, we have everything we need to bear fruit and live an abundant life. When worry threatens, we shift our focus.

ADORE

Let's explore how to do that a bit more.

EXPLORE

Read Philippians 4:4–9. What does this passage teach you about shifting your focus and turning your panic into praise?

What part does prayer play in helping us to let go of our worry?

What part does praising God play in helping us to let go of our worry?

Look back over the list mentioned in Philippians 4:8. Next to each word, write what you know to be true of God.

True

Noble

Right

Pure

Lovely

Admirable

Excellent

Praiseworthy

Read Matthew 11:28–30. What does this verse teach us about abiding in Christ and finding freedom from worry?

Read Jeremiah 17:7–8. Describe the person in this passage. What character traits mark the life of a person of great faith?

How might praising and adoring Christ help you to feel more rooted and calm? Why do you think that praise is so powerful in quieting our fears?

REFLECT

What is the difference between feeling concerned and feeling worried?

What typically triggers you to worry?

How might turning your panic into praise help calm your anxiety?

How does being connected to the vine quiet worry and fear?

Go back and consider Jesus' question, "Can you add to your life
by worrying?"

How does understanding that Jesus is the vine and you are a branch
help you answer His question?

PRAISE

Make a list of character traits of God that you know to be true. Then use your list as a guide for your praise time. Next to each character trait, write a short prayer to quiet your worry. For example:

- I praise You, God, that You are good. I don't need to worry, because Your plans for me are good.

- Lord, I praise You that You are loving. Thank You that You love my child even more than I do, and I can lay every worry at Your feet.

- Lord Jesus, I praise You that You are the vine. Thank You that I only have to be the branch.

has no one returned to give praise to God?

"Has no one returned to give praise to God
except this foreigner?"

LUKE 17:18

I AM THE LIVING ONE—THE FIRST AND THE LAST

When I saw him, I fell at his feet as though dead.
Then he placed his right hand on me and said: "Do not be
afraid. I am the First and the Last."

REVELATION 1:17

WEEK 8 | DAY 1

HAS NO ONE RETURNED TO GIVE PRAISE TO GOD?

LUKE 17:18

God's command to be thankful is not the threatening demand of a tyrant.
Rather, it is the invitation of a lifetime—
the opportunity to draw near to Him at any moment of the day.
—Nancy DeMoss Wolgemuth

Several years ago, Steve and I were traveling in Africa. While we were traipsing around Senegal, we were invited to have tea in a leper village. I felt a hesitation in my spirit. Lepers were still shunned in Senegal and had to live separately from the rest of their families. I had heard the disease was very contagious, and I wasn't quite sure how to respond. But my fearless husband, Steve, was not worried at all. I, on the other hand, had heard horror stories of leprosy. My mind wrestled with the horror of the disease versus the sweet hospitality of the villagers. Hand sanitizer in tow, we went to tea, and it was lovely. I have rarely been welcomed as graciously nor thanked as much for attending a village tea.

In case you're unfamiliar with leprosy, here's what I've discovered. Leprosy is an infectious disease that causes severe, disfiguring skin sores and nerve damage in the arms, legs, and skin areas of the body. Since ancient times, leprosy has been surrounded by negative stigmas, and patients are often shunned as outcasts. While leprosy is not highly contagious, it can be spread through the nose and mouth droplets of an untreated person.[22]

My hand sanitizer probably did nothing but make me feel better. As I left the village that day, my mind traveled back to the story of Jesus and the ten lepers and Jesus' question:

Has no one returned to give praise to God?

EXPLORE

Read Luke 17:11–19. Write your observations in the space below.

Read Luke 17:12. Circle the words "They stood at a distance."

Read Leviticus 13:45.

According to Old Testament law, lepers had to yell "unclean" whenever they were out so that people would have a warning to stay away.

This law would have been followed in the Jewish culture in which Jesus lived. Can you imagine declaring this about yourself wherever you went? Lepers couldn't enjoy loving touch from anyone, even those closest to them. They lived separate from their entire clan. What a sad and lonely life!

Read Luke 17:13. Instead of yelling "unclean" when Jesus and His followers came close, what did the men with leprosy yell out instead? Write it here:

Read Luke 17:14. Why do you think Jesus told the lepers to go show themselves to the priest?

Circle the words in this verse that say "As they went, they were cleansed."

I find those words significant because the lepers didn't see the healing until they obeyed what Jesus asked them to do. They had to obey by faith. The priests would not want to see them unless they had been completely healed! Often, we don't see the answers to our prayers until we've obeyed by faith.

Read Luke 17:15–16. Describe the response of the one leper who came back to Jesus. What adjectives would you use to describe his thanksgiving?

Read Luke 17:17–19. Jesus asked three questions. Write each question in the space below.

REFLECT

Think about your life. How has Jesus saved you, healed you, redeemed you, and set you free?

Beyond just gratitude, the leper fell at Jesus' feet and worshiped Him. Beyond Sunday morning, what does it look like for you to prioritize worshiping and praising Jesus Christ?

How might praising God and giving Him thanks deepen your faith?

PRAISE

Listen to "Praises" by Josh Baldwin. As you listen, praise Jesus Christ for all He is in your life and for all He has done in your life.

THE ONE WHO STILL LIVES

Praise is the catalyst
that speeds up God's maturing process in our lives.
— Ruth Myers

Yesterday we studied the story of the ten lepers, and we looked at how remarkable it was that out of ten lepers, only one returned and fell on his knees before Jesus to give Him thanks. Jesus asked, "Were not all ten cleansed? Where are the other nine? Has no one returned to give praise to God except this foreigner?" (Luke 17:17). That last question cuts to the core of who we are, doesn't it?

We've journeyed through this study. We've explored the depths of who Jesus Christ is and what He has done for us. Remember He is the great I Am. He is our Messiah, our Bread of Life, our Good Shepherd, our Light, and our Resurrection and Life. He is the Way, the Truth, and the Life, and He is our Vine. As we close our study this week, we're going to look at the truth that Jesus is still alive! He is the Living One—the First and the Last.

If you've explored other religions, you know that no other religion has a savior who is still alive. Every other religious prophet has a marker on their grave, except Jesus! Because He is alive! He has conquered sin, death, and hell because He has provided a way for us to live eternally with Him. The question, then, is how can we not fall at His feet and worship Him?

For the remainder of our study, we're going to look at making worship and praise a priority in our lives. Let's take a look at Jesus' statement to John in light of His question.

Has no one returned to give praise to God?
I Am the Living One!

EXPLORE

Read Revelation 1:8–17.

Before we unpack this, let me give you a little background. When John wrote the book of Revelation, he was an old man. He wrote the book during a time of extreme persecution for the church. In fact, John had been banished to the Greek island of Patmos because of His faith and testimony for Jesus Christ. From his banishment came this prophetic book.

John was able to say to other believers who were being persecuted for their faith that he was their companion in suffering. He had suffered greatly. In fact, church history teaches that John had been captured in Ephesus and thrown into a cauldron of burning oil. He miraculously survived and was then banished to the island of Patmos.[23] The island of Patmos is in the southern part of the Aegean Sea.

In the beginning of this book, I shared about my personal crisis of faith. I experienced suffering, although it was nothing compared to John's suffering. At one time or another, each of us will have suffering and sorrow of some kind. When suffering comes, we have a choice. We can run to Christ or away from Him. The chaos God allowed in my life became a catalyst, driving me to center my life completely on one thing—knowing Christ more.

John experienced horrific suffering, but he continually ran toward Christ. Even though he was in exile for his faith and had been persecuted, he worshiped Jesus. In fact, he was deep in worship when Jesus came to him in a vision. John wrote that when the vision happened, he was "in the Spirit." In other words, John was worshiping and in sync with the Spirit of God. One of the key components of worship is that when we truly worship, the Holy Spirit brings our spirit into perfect unity with God's spirit, and so we are able to say like John, "I was in the Spirit."

Read Revelation 1:12–16. While John is "in the Spirit," he has one incredible vision—Jesus appears to him. Describe the appearance of Jesus found in these verses.

Read Revelation 1:17–18. Describe John's response in verse 17. How is it similar to the response of the leper in Luke 17:16?

Read Revelation 1:18. Write Jesus' powerful *I Am* statement in the space below.

What are the implications of Jesus being eternally alive?

What do you think it means when Jesus said, "I hold the keys of death and Hades"?

REFLECT

What does Jesus' statement "I am alive forever and ever!" mean to you personally?

Read Hebrews 13:15. Describe what you think a "sacrifice of praise" is.

When you face a personal crisis, do you feel it's inauthentic to worship? Why or why not?

What part do you feel your emotions play in genuine worship?

What benefits do you see in developing an attitude of gratitude?

PRAISE

Listen to "So Will I (100 Billion X)" by Amanda Cook. As you listen, spend time simply praising God.

WHY DOES GOD INVITE US TO WORSHIP HIM?

What people revere, they resemble, either for ruin or for restoration.
—Greg Beale

Often people ask, "Why does God desire that we worship Him in the first place? Is He some insecure egotist who needs an 'attaboy' all the time to continue being God?"

Today, we're going to explore the answer to that question. But before we do, let's talk about what worship means. In the Old Testament, the word "worship" in the Hebrew meant to "bow down."[24] In the New Testament, the word "worship" means to "adore."[25]

You were designed in God's image with a desire to worship the God who created you. Think about it. You will worship and set something at the center of your life. God knows that we become like what we worship.

I believe we need to be captivated and centered on Christ! As we put Him at the very center of our lives, we bow to Him, we adore Him, we praise Him, we thank Him, and we obey Him. We become captivated, consumed, and controlled by Him. Our hearts long for what He longs for, our souls weep with what makes Him weep, and our desires are shaped around what He desires. When He is at the center of our lives, everything else will flow out of that center.

EXPLORE

Authentic worship transforms you and makes you more like Jesus.

Here are a few ways that praise transforms us:

1. Praise and worship elevate your view of God.

Read Revelation 1:12–17 and Isaiah 6:1–7. Write your observations in the space below, comparing John's vision with Isaiah's vision.

What are the similarities between John's response and Isaiah's response?

The more our view of God is elevated, the deeper our trust in His character grows. I'm reminded of the words I heard in a message from well-known contemporary preacher Francis Chan: "When we dwell on the greatness of God, we're overwhelmed by worship."

As we're praising and worshiping God, the Holy Spirit shifts our thinking and deepens our faith.

2. Praise and worship calm your fears and increase your faith.

Remember the principle you learned in Week 7? When fear, anxiety, or worry begin to attack your mind, shift your focus to what you know to be true about God, and your fears will be quieted. Turn your panic into praise.

3. Praise and worship open your ears to hear the voice of the Holy Spirit.

Read Acts 13:1–3. How did the disciples know they were to set apart Paul and Barnabas for missionary work?

4. Praise and worship defeat the enemy.

Read 2 Chronicles 20:1–24. What happened as soon as the people began to sing and praise the Lord for the splendor of His holiness?

REFLECT

Read Hebrews 12:2. How might fixing your eyes on and worshiping Jesus Christ deepen your faith in His sufficiency even during times of crisis?

In your life, how have praise and worship impacted your ability to hear God's voice?

PRAISE

Listen to "You Deserve It All" by Josh Baldwin. As you listen, praise Jesus Christ that the highest praise belongs to Him. You can borrow the words of the apostle Paul in Philippians 2:9–11: "Therefore, God exalted him to the highest place and gave him the name that is above every name, that at the name of Jesus every knee should bow, in heaven and on earth and under the earth, and every tongue acknowledge that Jesus Christ is Lord, to the glory of God the Father."

WEEK 8 | DAY 4

HOW?

We will find that the practice and discipline of worship
is the starting place for all of life in Christ,
for it determines to whom we yield and what we will prioritize.
—Jack Hayford

Worship has become a huge part of my spiritual journey. As I began to be intentional about worshiping Jesus Christ every morning, the Holy Spirit began to radically change my life. Fear turned to courage, worry turned to calm, and doubt turned to faith. I now believe that becoming intentional in the realm of praise is essential for every believer.

In the midst of schedules, deadlines, and demands, you might be wondering, "How in the world am I supposed to find time to worship? And besides, isn't that what I do on Sunday morning? Isn't Sunday worship enough?"

Today, I'd like to give you some practical tips to cultivate the private art of worship. As you put these tips into practice, I guarantee your life will change. It's simply impossible to worship Jesus Christ and not be changed! Let's begin by looking at some simple tools you can use to cultivate your worship time, and then we'll look at how to carve out time to actually do it.

EXPLORE

Read Psalm 149. What tangible tools do you see listed in this passage that you could use to enhance your times of personal worship?

Tool #1—Music

Read Psalm 149:3. Circle the phrase "make music" in your Bible.

The phrase "make music" that's used here in the Hebrew is *zamar*. It means to make music and sing praises, to sing songs accompanied by musical instruments. The phrase occurs more than 45 times throughout the Psalms (Strong's #2167).

In our culture today, we have tools like YouTube, iTunes, Vimeo, and other places that allow us to listen to all the new worship music that's being created and recorded every day. What a gift! Worship songs can help to lead your heart into a mood of praise and worship. They can create an atmosphere of praise and positivity in your home. So here's my suggestion—create a play list of music that fits your style. There's tons of music available out there, so do some research and find music that you love. If you have kids, find music that they'll love and you can enjoy together.

List at least six songs that you love to get your play list started:

Tool #2—Scripture

Read Psalm 149:6.

When the psalmist talks about the double-edged sword, he is referring
to Scripture. Several times in Scripture, the Word of God is referred
to as a sword. This is because using the Word of God is a powerful
weapon against the enemy of our souls, Satan. When you praise God
and use Scripture, Satan flees. Learn to bring God's Word into your
praise time. There are several ways to do this.

- Use different psalms of praise, and as you are praising God,
  borrow the language of the psalmist.
- Use the different blessings and benedictions of the apostle Paul,
  including passages such as Ephesians 3:20–21 or Philippians
  2:9–11.
- Use the different doxologies found in the book of Revelation,
  such as Revelation 5:12, Revelation 5:13, or Revelation 4:8.
- Use the *I Am* statements of Jesus, and praise your way through
  them.

Create a list of at least five Scripture passages that you will begin to incorporate into your praise time.

Tool #3—Creation

Read Psalm 148. What does this psalm teach you about creation worshiping God?

The beauty of God's creation can prompt your praise. At some point in your day, if you're able, take a walk outside. Walk in silence, but observe the beauty of God's creation, and simply praise God for all that you experience through your five senses.

Tool #4—Journal

Keeping a "thankful" list, especially during stressful seasons of life, can be very helpful. I remember during a particularly stressful and chaotic season writing down three things or events that I felt thankful for before bed each night. The result was that I slept better and woke up with a positive attitude.

Another way to use your journal is to write out a prayer of praise every day. On top of cultivating your praise journey, you'll have a written record of all that you feel thankful for. When life feels hard, you can read back over your prayers and find encouragement.

CARVING OUT THE TIME TO WORSHIP

When you look at your daily schedule, you might instantly feel overwhelmed. But here are a few suggestions for times during the day you can create the space for worship.

When you first wake up

Rather than catapulting out of bed worrying about the demands of the day, lie in bed and listen to a worship song. Praise God for a new day. Or make coffee and spend ten minutes worshiping and praising God while you drink that first cup of coffee.

Set aside your car time

Most of us spend time every day driving. Rather than chatting on your phone, play some music while you drive and spend your car time praising God. I guarantee this will make your work commute less stressful. If you're raising kids, after you drop them at school or soccer, spend your drive home praising God for each child. You'll find your car time far less annoying and much more life giving.

During your lunch break

Most of us take time for lunch. After you eat, take a walk and spend a few short moments worshiping God for all He is doing in your life.

Before you fall asleep at night

Rather than stressing about all that went wrong throughout your day, praise God for His faithfulness. Use some of the Scriptures you've put in your toolbox.

REFLECT

How might your life change if you begin to prioritize praising God?

Look back over the list of tools I gave you. Which tool do you feel might be most effective in prompting your praise?

Sunday morning worship is important but so are individual times of worship. How might you rearrange your schedule so that you could free up 15–30 minutes daily to intentionally praise God?

MEMORIZE

Write out the words to Psalm 150.

PRAISE

Listen to the "New Doxology" by Gateway Worship and Thomas Miller. As you listen, praise Jesus Christ using His *I Am* statements. For example, "I praise You, Jesus, because You are the Messiah, the one who came to heal my guilt."

After you've praised through all the *I Am* statements of Jesus, then listen to "Praise Will be My Song" by Bryan and Katie Torwalt. As you listen, make it your commitment to make praise your song as you move through the rest of your life. May the wonder of Jesus Christ so fill your heart that your entire life will be one continuous praise song.

FALL AT HIS FEET

Remember my crisis of faith that I told you about at the beginning of this study? Every crisis of faith is an opportunity to re-evaluate and strengthen faith. Looking back, I'm thankful for that season even though at the time it felt very dark. I'm grateful that I decided to re-evaluate my faith rather than settling for pat answers. I'm thrilled that I reanalyzed every question and statement Jesus made because now, when He asks me, "Becky, but you, who do you say I am?", with resounding faith I boldly declare,

"You ARE the Christ, the Son of the living God!"

That certainty has changed everything for me. It is what gets me up in the morning and what tucks my thoughts into bed at night. It is what compels me to hop on airplanes and fly all over the world (at times to places I'm not fond of going) so that others can hear of the incredible love of Christ. It is what gives my life purpose and passion. And it is what drives me to my knees in His presence and compels me to cry out, "You are worthy of all my praise!"

So what about you, friend? Where are you at after considering Jesus' questions and encountering Him through His *I Am* statements? Are you ready to fall at His feet and boldly declare, "You are the Christ, the Son of the Living God!"?

Today is our last day. I'm a little sad that our time together is over. Endings can feel a bit painful. But, hey, let's not think of today as a goodbye! I'd hate for you to close the book and say, "Well, that was a fun study, but it's done and now what's next?" Instead, before you close the book, I want you to consider what you've learned, how you've changed, and what will be different as you move forward in your life.

So here's the deal, today I'm going to lead you through some reflective questions to help you consider how you've changed and where you'd like to go from here. I'm a big believer in processing. If you don't process how you've changed, the transformation likely won't last. Let's get started.

WHAT DID YOU LEARN?

As you reflect back on this study, which of Jesus' questions did you most relate to and why?

What did you learn about how Jesus used questions as a method of helping people realize greater truth?

As you reflect on Jesus' *I Am* statements, which statement felt the most transformational for you? What specifically made it so profound for you? How did that statement deepen your faith in Christ's identity?

What did you learn about the concept of "believing" as a result of this study?

What did you learn that was new and faith-building as a result of doing this study?

HOW HAVE YOU CHANGED?

Think back to the beginning of the study. What was the condition of your faith? Describe where you were spiritually in the space below.

Describe what you believe to be true about Jesus Christ. If Jesus were to ask you, "Who do *you* say that I Am?", how would you answer after completing this study?

When trials and suffering come our way, it's easy to doubt God's goodness and love. After completing this study, what tools do you have for seasons of suffering to help you keep your faith strong and healthy?

Now that you have completed this study, list any changes you have observed or others have observed in you, especially in the realm of attitude.

WHERE WILL YOU GO FROM HERE?

Friend, life with Jesus Christ is an abundant adventure! My prayer for you is that you've grown more confident in your faith, more secure in His love, more assured of His goodness, and more bold about sharing His story. It can be helpful to set some goals for yourself as far as where you go from here. For example, maybe you've realized as a result of completing this study that you need to continue memorizing Scripture. You might set a goal of memorizing one or two new verses per week as a part of your daily routine. Or maybe you've enjoyed listening to worship music during this study, and you realize how faith-building worship is and so you might set aside 15–30 minutes per day to start listening to worship music. Develop a worship playlist of your top five favorite worship songs.

Set some goals for yourself for how you'd like to continue building your faith.

PRAISE

As we close out this Bible study, I think it's fitting to end by having you listen to "This I Believe (The Creed)" by Hillsong Worship. As you listen, make this your bold declaration of faith! Praise God that your faith in Jesus Christ is reasonable and built on solid evidence that is able to stand the tests of time and trials.

After you've listened to "This I Believe," listen to "Praise Will be My Song" by Bryan and Katie Torwalt. As you listen, make it your commitment to make praise your song as you move through the rest of your life.

May the wonder of Jesus Christ fill your heart so completely that your entire life will be one continuous praise song!

DEAR FRIEND. . .

I pray that you have enjoyed *Who Do You Say that I Am?* I pray that your faith has gone deeper than you ever could have imagined, that you are at a point of being "all in," and that you will walk away from this Bible study with your life completely centered on Jesus Christ.

The crisis of faith I wrote about in the first week certainly became a catalyst for me to center my life on Jesus Christ. Once He becomes the absolute center of your life, you are willing to surrender everything to Him. The call to follow Him becomes your single quest. You live to hear His voice and to obey His every command. You worship, adore, and praise Him with every fiber of your being because you realize He gave everything for you.

It's not that you never have doubts again. Those will continue to come because we are human, but in your times of doubt, you can return to the fact that you studied and considered Christ's claims and concluded that He is exactly who He said He was, the Son of the living God. God Himself! As a result of that conviction, you begin to realize that even when trials come and He allows deep soul stripping, in the end He gives Himself, and that, my friend, is worth everything!

I have loved journeying through the *I Am* statements with you, so I'm hoping we'll stay connected. You might enjoy some of the other books I've written: *Rewriting Your Emotional Script, Freedom from Performing, The 30 Day Praise Challenge, The 30 Day Praise Challenge for Parents*, and *How to Listen So People Will Talk*. You can receive my most recent blog posts in your inbox each week by signing up at www.beckyharling.com.

You can also follow me on:

Facebook: www.facebook.com/beckyharlingministries

Twitter: @BeckyHarling

LinkedIn: www.linkedin.com/in/becky-harling-31605212

Instagram: BeckyHarling

iTunes: A new podcast, "Beyond Beautiful!", inspiring women to be the voice and hands of Jesus in their world.

Blessings and joy to you,

Becky Harling

Becky Harling

NOTES

1. Robert L. Deffinbaugh, "10. The Woman at the Well (John 4:1-42)," Bible.org, August 19, 2004, https://bible.org/seriespage/10-woman-well-john-41-42.

2. All "Strong's Exhaustive Concordance Online" citations in the book can be found here: http://www.biblestudytools.com/concordances/strongs exhaustive concordance/.

3. "What is the conviction of sin?" GotQuestions.org, https://www.gotquestions .org/conviction-of-sin.html.

4. "Sea of Galilee," Wikipedia, s.v. "Sea of Galilee," last modified September 16, 2017, 03:37, https://en.wikipedia.org/wiki/Sea_of_Galilee.

5. W.E. Vine, *An Expository Dictionary of New Testament Words* (Old Tappan, NJ: Fleming H. Revell Company, 1966), 116.

6. Ruth Myers, *The Satisfied Heart: 31 Days of Experiencing God's Love* (Colorado Springs: Waterbrook Press, 1999), 45.

7. Beth Moore, *Audacious* (Nashville: B&H Publishing Group, 2015), 149.

8. "Reflections February 2014—God's Gift-love and Our Need-love," *C.S. Lewis Institute*, January 28, 2014, http://www.cslewisinstitute.org/Gods_Gift_love_ and_Our_Need_love.

9. Philip W. Comfort and Wendell C. Hawley, *Opening the Gospel of John* (Wheaton, IL: Tyndale, 1994), 111.

10. Dorothy Kelly Patterson, ed., "Chart on Names of God," *The Women's Study Bible* (Nashville: Nelson, 1995), 861.

11. See note 10 above.

12. Michael J. Wilkins, "Darkness," Bible Study Tools, http://www.biblestudytools .com/dictionary/darkness/.

13. Brennan Manning, *Ruthless Trust: The Ragamuffin's Path to God* (New York: Harper Collins, 2009), 3.

14. Larry Crabb, *Shattered Dreams: God's Unexpected Pathway to Joy* (Colorado Springs: Waterbrook, 2001), 144.

15. Vance Christie, "'In Time of Trouble Say' (Andrew Murray)," vancechristie.com, August 29, 2015, http://www.vancechristie.com/2015/08/29/in-time-of-trouble-say-andrew-murray/.

16. R.C. Sproul, *John (St. Andrew's Expositional Commentary)* (Lake Mary, FL: Reformation Trust Publishing, 2009), 269–72.

17. Bruce B. Barton, Philip W. Comfort, David R. Veerman, Neil Wilson, *Life Application Bible Commentary* (Wheaton, IL: Tyndale House Publishers, Inc., 1993), 305.

18. John F. Hart, "John," in T*he Moody Bible Commentary*, Michael Rydelnik and Michael Vanlaningham, eds. (Chicago: Moody Publishers, 2014), 1650.

19. Bruce Wilkinson, *Secrets of the Vine* (Sisters, OR: Multnomah, 2001), 33.

20. Hart, *The Moody Bible Commentary*, Rydelnik and Vanlaningham, eds., 1650.

21. Heather Holleman, *Seated with Christ* (Chicago: Moody Publishers, 2015), 113–114.

22. "Leprosy Overview," WebMD, http://www.webmd.com/skin-problems-and-treatments/guide/leprosy-symptoms-treatments-history#1.

23. "How did the apostle John die?" GotQuestions.org, https://www.gotquestions.org/apostle-John-die.html.

24. Michael Morrison, "What Is Worship? A Survey of Scripture," Grace Communion International, https://www.gci.org/God/worship.

25. "4576. sebó," Bible Hub, http://biblehub.com/greek/4576.htm.

ACKNOWLEDGMENTS

MY SPECIAL THANKS TO:

My husband, Steve. Babe, thanks for always believing in and supporting me in the ministry that God has called me to do. You've continually challenged me to go further, to step into the calling God has placed on my life. I love the adventure we're living together as we seek to be the voice and hands of Jesus around the world! I love you!

MY KIDS:

Bethany, what a joy to see you step more fully into your ministry of adoption and foster care. Watching you grow deeper in trusting God and stepping out by faith into uncharted territory has been such a joy! Your heart mirrors God's heart for the least of these. I love you, Bethany!

Josiah, I love watching your leadership flourish and thrive as you continue to follow God's call on your life in ministry. You have an extraordinary ability to motivate and move churches toward missions, and it's been incredible for me as your Mom to watch! I deeply respect your prayer life and the way you intentionally pray Scripture over your family. I love you, JJ!

Stefanie, oh how I love your heart for the Word. I remember even as a little girl watching you open your Bible and underline verses that you could read. I remember watching you as a teen dive into the Word for comfort and hope when Dad and I were walking through such great difficulties in the church we were serving. And now, watching you as a parent teach your kids and others the Word is extraordinary. Your passion is contagious! I'm so proud of you and I love you, Stef!

Kerith, what an incredible worship leader you are. Watching you minister both from the platform as a worship leader and in your home as you encourage and mentor others has brought me incredible joy. Your sweet spirit and joyful attitude touch everyone who knows you. I love you, Keri!

MY KIDS-IN-LOVE:

Chris, you model the servant heart of Jesus better than anyone I know. Watching you love Bethany and your boys brings me to tears. You're such a godly, gentle husband and father. I have loved watching you and Bethany take risks for the kingdom and step out by faith in the realms of adoption and foster care. I love you, Chris!

Shaina, wow, when I dreamed of having a daughter-in-law, I never imagined she would be as wonderful as you are! Your gentleness and godliness are extraordinary. I love your heart for prayer. Your sweet, calm spirit is beautiful. I love you, Shainey!

Dave, I have loved watching your leadership develop as God has called you to greater levels of influence at work. What a joy to see how you share Christ with others in such a gentle and transparent way. I love watching you encourage Stef to use her gifts and I love how you take each of your kids on dates. I love you, Dave!

Zach, I love your passion for being a godly leader. You have extraordinary gifts in leadership and influencing others. You are so intentional in your walk with Christ, and it is evident in all you do! I'm so thankful for your love for Keri and your kids. What a joy to watch you parent! I love you, Zach!

MY GRANDKIDS:

Charlie, what a joy to watch you confidently grow in your love for Jesus and His Word. Papa and I are proud of you and love you so much!

Tyler, I love your sensitive heart to Jesus and to hear His voice. I love how you're already writing worship songs! Papa and I are proud of you and love you so much!

Joshua, I love how you are strong and courageous for Jesus. Your confidence in stepping into new situations is extraordinary. Papa and I are so proud of you and love you tons!

Selah, I love how you sparkle and shine for Jesus. You are kind and sweet and love others so well! Papa and I are so proud of you and love you so much!

Zachary, I love how you are learning to be strong and courageous for Jesus. What a little world changer you are! God's got big plans for you, buddy! Papa and I are so proud of you and love you tons!

Theo, I love your sense of humor and how you have such an adventurous spirit. Wow, do you make me laugh! I know God has big plans for you! Papa and I are so proud of you and love you so very much!

Noah, I love your exuberance and passion for life. Your people skills are already extraordinary! I know God has a special calling on your life. Papa and I are so proud of you and love you so much!

Rayna, I love your joy and the way you light up the room. You are such a little sweetheart, and Papa and I are so proud of you and love you tons!

Cayden, I love your determination and your sweet spirit. Watching you with your brothers and cousins is an absolute joy. Papa and I are so proud of you and love you so much!

Kinley, I love what a sweet and contented baby you are. Your big blue eyes sparkle and shine. Sweetie, Papa and I love you so much!

Baby Victoria, your name means victory! Mimi and Papa praise God for you precious little one! May you grow up to love Jesus.

ALL THE MEN AND WOMEN WHO MADE THIS BOOK POSSIBLE:

Judy Dunagan, thanks for being my dear friend in addition to being the acquisitions editor for this book. What a joy to work together with you on this project! I'm so thankful for the years of friendship and all the times we've been on our knees together. I love you, friend!

Blythe Daniel, thanks for being my dear friend and agent! Thanks for believing in this project and cheering me on. I love that beyond being my agent you have become a dear friend!

Amanda Cleary Eastep, thanks for being such a gentle and kind developmental editor. It's been so fun to get to know you!

All the men and women at Moody Publishers, thanks for your heart for God's Word. What a joy to be published by you!

Rebecca Pickard, my incredible intern! Rebecca, you are a rock star, and I am so thankful for all you do for me. I love working with you!

To our incredible assistant, Lani Hawes—Lani, thank you so much for managing my schedule, for helping Steve and I stay on track, and for reading through all the Scriptures in this study! I'm so thankful for you!

The incredible men and women who serve alongside us at Reach Beyond. What a joy and incredible privilege to serve together as we make Christ known among the least reached.

New Bible Studies for Women

FROM MOODY PUBLISHERS

978-0-8024-1468-7

978-0-8024-1473-1

978-0-8024-1742-8

978-0-8024-1467-0

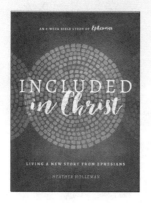

978-0-8024-1591-2

978-0-8024-1596-7

978-0-8024-1686-5

MOODY PUBLISHERS
WOMEN
BIBLE STUDIES

IN-DEPTH.
CHRIST-CENTERED.
REAL IMPACT.

Also available as eBooks

Discipleship Resources

FROM MOODY PUBLISHERS

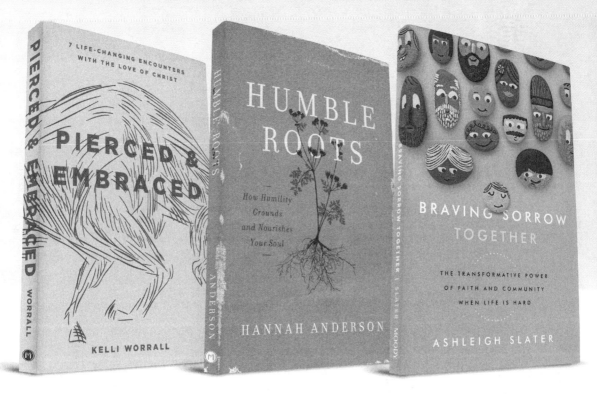

978-0-8024-1631-5   978-0-8024-1459-5   978-0-8024-1659-9

Moody Publishers is committed to providing powerful, biblical, and life-changing discipleship resources for women. Our prayer is that these resources will cause a ripple effect of making disciples who make disciples who make disciples.

Also available as eBooks